AUGUST WILSON

August Wilson. (Photograph by Glen Frieson)

AUGUST WILSON

A Research and Production Sourcebook

YVONNE SHAFER

Modern Dramatists Research and Production Sourcebooks, Number 14
William W. Demastes, Series Adviser

Greenwood Press
Westport, Connecticut • London

Library of Congress Cataloging-in-Publication Data

Shafer, Yvonne, 1936–
    August Wilson : a research and production sourcebook / Yvonne
Shafer.
      p.   cm.—(Modern dramatists research and production
sourcebooks, ISSN 1055–999X ; no. 14)
    Includes bibliographical references (p.   ) and index.
    ISBN 0–313–29270–1 (alk. paper)
    1. Wilson, August—Criticism and interpretation. 2. Historical
drama, American—History and criticism. 3. Afro-Americans in
literature—Bibliography. 4. Afro-Americans in literature.
5. Wilson, August—Bibliography. I. Title. II. Series.
PS3573.I45677Z87   1998
812′.54—dc21   97–38989

British Library Cataloguing in Publication Data is available.

Library of Congress Catalog Card Number: 97–38989
ISBN: 0–313–29270–1
ISSN: 1055–999X

First published in 1998

Greenwood Press, 88 Post Road West, Westport, CT 06881
An imprint of Greenwood Publishing Group, Inc.

Printed in the United States of America

The paper used in this book complies with the
Permanent Paper Standard issued by the National
Information Standards Organization (Z39.48–1984).

10 9 8 7 6 5 4 3 2 1

Contents

CONTENTS

Acknowledgments

My thanks to Louis Rachow of the International Theatre Institute. He was, as always, extraordinarily generous and helpful. Fred Wilkins, Tom Shafer, Susan Kelley, Don Marlette, Sister Ellen Frawley, and Ron Willis gave me valuable encouragement and suggestions. Lucie Miller and the staff of the Rochester Public Library were very helpful and forthcoming and assisted me in locating articles in some obscure journals. Nena Couch, Curator of the Jerome Lawrence and Robert E. Lee Theatre Research Institute, ever efficient and knowledgeable, sent me information about the 1996 William Inge Festival dedicated to August Wilson. Jon Quist of the Computer Laboratory at St. John's University, Staten Island, came to my aid whenever I had problems. My chairperson at St. John's University, Dr. Gloria Seminara, kindly assisted me in obtaining a teaching load reduction so I could finish the book. I am grateful for the advice and assistance of my editor, William W. Demastes. The staff of the New York Public Library for the Performing Arts Research Collections helped me with research at all stages of the writing. I was grateful for information about the history of jazz and *Ma Rainey's Black Bottom* given to me by jazz historian Eugene Kramer. He and his wife, Carol, warmed my life in an otherwise cold and lonely Rochester winter. David and Carolyn Schuler kindly gave me the use of their computer, apartment, and library so that I was able to take a leave of absence from teaching overseas and return to the United States to finish the book. Sandra Hollischer, Communications Director of the Penumbra Theatre, and Martha Bowden, Press Representative for Yale Repertory Theatre, spent time collecting and sending articles and reviews which were difficult to obtain. Likewise, Stephen Pitalo of Boneau/Bryan-Brown sent me last-minute press releases and other information about the opening of *Seven Guitars* in New York. Laurel Saiz, Press Representative for the

Syracuse Repertory, arranged tickets for a very exciting production of *The Piano Lesson*. I was grateful for the time August Wilson gave me in taping a lengthy interview and helping me with up-to-date information in 1997. Numerous actors, including Kim Sullivan, gave me information regarding their performances in Wilson plays and their work with him. It was generous of Jim Ponds, a marvelous Wining Boy in the production, to give me an interview between a matinee and an evening performance of that very demanding play. Many of the people assisted me because of their great admiration and affection for a wonderful playwright and a fine human being, August Wilson.

I am grateful, as always, for the encouragement of Professor Marvin Carlson of CUNY to whom this book is dedicated.

A Note on Codes
and Numbering

Extensive references in this book are arranged according to type of material and designated by a prefix and code number. Prefixes used for these listings are described below.

"A"--A prefix identifying primary, non-dramatic references, listed alphabetically and annotated in the "Primary Bibliography."

"P"--A prefix identifying productions of plays listed in "Productions and Credits."

"R" and "S"--Descriptive prefixes identifying reviews ("R") and other secondary materials ("S"). These references and annotations are chronologically combined and located in numerical sequence in the "Secondary Bibliography."

Chronology

1945   Born 27 April to Daisy Wilson Kittel and Frederick Kittel on Bedford Avenue in a racially mixed part of Pittsburgh. Given name is Freddy August Kittel. Father is a white German baker. Family receives welfare and mother does janitorial work.

1959   Stepfather, David Bedford, moves family to white suburb.

1960-61   Racism in school. Wilson is accused of submitting a paper written by his sister and, as a result, drops out of Gladstone High School just after having entered the 10th grade.

1963   Wilson spends one year in army and then is discharged.

1965   Saves money from job and moves from mother's home to a rooming house in Pittsburgh. Buys his first typewriter. First hears a Bessie Smith recording. Writing poetry, encouraged by group of black artists. Death of natural father.

1968   Co-founder with Rob Penny of Black Horizons Theatre. Directs a play written by Penny. Inspired by a *Tulane Drama Review* devoted to black theatre.

1969   Marries Brenda Burton. Death of stepfather.

1970   Daughter Sakina Ansari-Wilson born.

1972   Breakdown of first marriage. Wilson finds some success as
                poet and gives poetry readings in local art galleries.

1976   Wilson sees his first professional play in a theatre. Moving
                toward playwriting. Inspired by Ma Rainey recording to
                begin work on *Ma Rainey's Black Bottom*.

1977   Writes musical satire *Black Bart and the Sacred Hills* at
                request of Claude Purdy for production in Minneapolis.

1978   Visits Penumbra Theatre in Minneapolis with Claude
                Purdy. Moves to Minneapolis/St. Paul. Works at Science
                Museum in Minneapolis writing plays for Children's
                Theatre. Sends script to Playwrights Center in
                Minneapolis, awarded a Jerome Fellowship, and becomes
                a member of group. Introduced to art of Romare Bearden.

1980   Works as cook for three years for Little Brothers of the
                Poor. Spends one-half of each day cooking and one-half
                writing plays and poetry.

1981   *Black Bart* is produced at Penumbra Theatre. Marries Judy
                Oliver. Develops early work on *Ma Rainey's Black Bottom*
                into full script. Submits it to O'Neill Center.

1982   *Ma Rainey's Black Bottom* given staged reading at O'Neill
                Center. Meets Lloyd Richards. Receives a Bush
                Fellowship. Wilson is able to devote himself fully to
                writing for the first time.

1983   Wilson's mother dies. *Fences* given a staged reading at
                O'Neill Center.

1984   *Ma Rainey's Black Bottom* performed at Yale Repertory
                Theatre (April). Play opens at Cort Theatre in New York

(October). Wilson granted Rockefeller Fellowship. Staged reading of *Joe Turner's Come and Gone* at O'Neill Center.

1985 *Ma Rainey's Black Bottom* receives Theatre of Renewal Award, then Drama Critics Circle Award and a Tony nomination for Best Play. McKnight Fellowship for Wilson. *Fences* opens at Yale Repertory Theatre (April).

1986 Wilson awarded a Whiting Foundation Award and a Guggenheim fellowship. *Joe Turner's Come and Gone* opens at Yale Repertory Theatre (April). Play was inspired by a painting by Romare Bearden.

1987 *Fences* opens at 46th St. Theatre in New York (Mar.). Wins all major awards including Pulitzer Prize, Drama Critics Circle Award, and Tony Award for Best Play. *The Piano Lesson* opens at Yale Repertory Theatre (Nov.). Play was also inspired by a painting by Romare Bearden.

1988 *Joe Turner's Come and Gone* opens at Ethel Barrymore Theatre in New York (March). New York Drama Critics Circle Award, Tony nomination for Best Play. Wilson's income is estimated at over $1 million a year. Described by critics as the foremost dramatist of the American black experience.

1990 *The Piano Lesson* opens at Walter Kerr Theatre in New York (April). Wins all major awards including Pulitzer Prize, Drama Critics Circle Award, and Tony Award for Best Play. *Two Trains Running* opens at Yale Repertory Theatre (March). Wilson's second marriage ends in divorce, and he moves to Seattle. Considered by many critics to be the most acclaimed playwright of his time.

1991 Selected for membership in the American Academy of Arts and Sciences.

1992 *Two Trains Running* opens at Walter Kerr Theatre in New York (April). Wins American Theatre Critics' Association

Award, Drama Critics Circle Award, and a Tony nomination for Best Play.

1993   Bush Artists Fellowship given to Wilson. Plans to write play for Olympics in Atlanta, 1996. Pursuing plays in his cycle, intending one play for each decade of the twentieth century.

1994   Wilson and costumer Constanza Romero are married.

1995   *Seven Guitars* produced at Goodman Theatre in Chicago (Jan.). *The Piano Lesson* presented on CBS television, Hallmark Hall of Fame (Jan.). Selected for membership in American Academy of Arts and Letters.

1996   *Seven Guitars* produced at Walter Kerr Theatre in New York (March). Wins several awards including Drama Critics Circle Award for Best Play and two Outer Critics Circle Awards. William Inge Festival (Kansas) dedicated to Wilson who addresses the participants.   Presents Keynote Address to Theatre Communications Group National Conference (June).

1997   Robert Brustein attacks Wilson's TCG speech. Wilson responds, and arguments between them lead to debate at New York's Town Hall with Anna Deavere Smith as moderator (Jan.). Overflow crowd attends debate and interrupts with heckling for both men. Wilson criticized by a number of writers and critics for "separatist" point of view. In residence at Crossroads Theater in New Jersey to revise early play *Jitney* for production in late spring. Writing a new play set in the 1980s about the disintegration of a black family in a violent age, called *King Hedley II*.

Life and Career

August Wilson is one of only seven American playwrights to win two Pulitzer Prizes and one of only three black playwrights to receive the prize. When *Ma Rainey's Black Bottom* opened in 1984, Wilson was completely unknown in the theatre. By 1988 he was described as the foremost dramatist of the American black experience and by 1990, the most acclaimed playwright of his time. In the following years he achieved such success that, as critic Paul Taylor (R139) has noted, "Wilson is the only contemporary dramatist, apart from Neil Simon, who is assured a Broadway production and his have been the pioneer black works at many regional theatres." He has won Rockefeller, Bush, McKnight, and Guggenheim Foundation fellowships in playwriting, and Tony Awards and Drama Critics Circle Awards. In 1988 he achieved the distinction of having two plays running on Broadway, *Fences* and *Joe Turner's Come and Gone*. His plays have been described as "powerful," "thrilling," and "explosive." Remarkably, Wilson has been able to explore and communicate the black experience in America in a way which seems particular to blacks and achieves a universality which has drawn the white audiences needed for a commercial success. He explores small lives in very particular places, but as critics have often noted, they are small people but they summon up a universe. Kroll (R164) wrote in 1995, "No black playwright has entered the mainstream as strongly as Wilson." Wilson's background, his approach to playwriting, and the stage history of his plays reveal a unique experience in the American theatre.

Wilson was born Freddy August Kittel in 1945 in Pittsburgh. His mother's maiden name was Wilson, which he later chose as his last name. He has given the names of some of his ancestors (Zonia, Bynum, Cutler) to the characters in his plays. He grew up in a racially mixed ghetto known as the Hill. There his home (now a boarded up, empty building) was at 1727 Bedford Avenue, above Bella's Grocery Store. His background seems an unlikely one to produce a highly successful poet and playwright. His family had little educational background and little money. The large family lived in two rooms with no hot water and with few comforts except a radio. His father was a white baker, Frederick Kittel. He was an infrequent presence in the household. He fathered August and five other children who remembered him largely as a hard drinking German who showed up occasionally with a bag of fresh baked rolls. In fact, he was an infrequent presence in the household, leaving the children a few memories and one photograph of him with three other white men. He died in 1965. His place was taken by Wilson's stepfather, David Bedford.

Wilson revered his mother who worked at a janitorial job, received welfare, and did her best to bring up the children so that they would have a chance in society. Despite her hardships she brought the children up with love and did whatever she could to make their lives happy. She would wait until Christmas Eve so she could buy a tree for $1.00. She also bought second-hand books including Nancy Drew books. Wilson remembers that she won a washing machine on a radio contest by giving her daughter a dime to run to the pay phone and call in the answer. But when the people found out she was black, they said she could have a certificate for a used machine from the Salvation Army, but not the new Speed Queen. Her pride caused her to tell them what she thought of them and keep on scrubbing on a washboard. That is Wilson's favorite story about his mother. Wilson said that his mother taught him to read when he was four. "She kept books around the house; it was very important. We had a time that we would all sit down and she would read a few pages and then she would let us go out and play." (S088) The first evidence Wilson gave of an interest in writing was in seventh grade when he wrote love poems to leave on a girl's desk. As a youth Wilson was taken to the Catholic church by a kind woman in the neighborhood whom he still speaks of with great affection.

Wilson suffered the effects of racism in America: when his family tried to move into a mostly white neighborhood, bricks were thrown through the windows. He frequently tells interviewers the troubles he encountered in school. He attended St. Stephen's parochial school where he was the only black student in his eighth grade class. He then attended Central Catholic High School where he was the only black in the school. His mother hoped he would graduate, go to college, and become a lawyer.

Unfortunately, the other students left racist notes on his desk telling him to leave and waited in the yard to beat him up. The principal would send him home in a cab, but he had to come to school by himself the next morning and face the same bullies. He got in many fights, and finally got tired of it and quit. His mother then sent him to the Connelly Trade School where he was supposed to learn automobile repair work. The classes for auto body were full when he arrived. So he was put into the sheet metal shop and only taught how to make cups from tin sheets. (He made the cups badly, but he used the knowledge later in *Joe Turner's Come and Gone.*) Some days he was supposed to have regular classes, but discovered that most of the students could barely read and the work was at about the fifth grade level, so he dropped out again. He then went to Gladstone High School, across the street from his home. In the short time that he was in 10th grade he became increasingly interested in history. Having written a long paper on Napoleon, he was outraged when he was accused by his black teacher of submitting a paper one of his older sisters had written for him. He told the teacher that, in fact, he wrote their papers for them. He felt it was enough to say that he wrote the paper. When the teacher didn't accept that and gave him back the paper, he tore it up and threw it in the trash basket. Again, he left school; this time he dropped out for good. At the age of fifteen he continued his education by spending his days in the library reading--especially in the section marked "Negro" where there were about thirty books. At that time the mere presence of books by black authors on the shelves was a comfort and he dreamed of having books of his own there. He wished he could have been a part of the Harlem Renaissance. When he wasn't in the library, Wilson was doing odd jobs and hanging around the streets and a cigar store/pool hall which was a center for interesting neighborhood characters.

His was the archetypal black American experience. From the street he learned a rich, vibrant argot which he would later transmute into powerful, striking language in his poems and plays. Pittsburgh locations such as the white-owned Lutz' Meat Store and Bella's Grocery are remembered in his plays. He began writing poetry, which concerned his mother because she did not think he could earn a living in that way. Denied what he calls "meaningful employment" because of discrimination, he worked as a short-order cook and a store clerk. He saw scenes of violence including that of blacks against blacks which he has put into his plays. He lived at home, but did not get along with his stepfather. Later, he came to an understanding of the difficult life the man had faced, including 23 years in prison, and he felt that the generation of his mother and his stepfather had tried to shield their children from the brutal realities of racism. His stepfather died in 1969 but his mother lived until 1983.

In 1965 Wilson saved some money and moved from his mother's home. At the age of twenty he was living in a Pittsburgh rooming house along with a retired counterfeiter, a convicted arsonist, and a would-be singer, among others. He was a close observer of the life around him and remembers such things as a woman called Miss Sarah who sprinkled salt and lined up pennies across her threshhold. He savored the stories told by the men in the neighborhood and asked questions about life and death of people they discussed (S050). Critics have often noted the importance of story telling in his plays. He bought his first typewriter for $20 and slowly learned to type. An important element in his life was the proximity of the St. Vincent de Paul store where he bought a record player for $3 and began to buy old 78 rpm records for 5 cents each. Ultimately, he had a collection of about 2,000 records--a virtual history of popular music and blues. One day he heard Bessie Smith sing "Nobody in Town Can Bake A Sweet Jelly Roll Like Mine" and was stunned by its beauty and honesty. This was his discovery of the blues as a cultural heritage and that concept became a central element in his work.

At this same time he was involved with a group of black writers, intellectuals, and political activists who helped shape his life and give it meaning. Rob Penny, a writer-teacher, and others encouraged him in his writing and he read his poems at art shows and galleries. With Penny he co-founded the Black Horizons Theatre. Penny had written a play and Wilson, with no experience, successfully directed it. Inspired by an issue of the *Tulane Drama Review* devoted to black theatre, he tried to write a play. He was influenced by the many things he had read, including poetry by Dylan Thomas and John Berryman, and he was excited by the dialogue in Amiri Baraka's plays. He married Brenda Burton in 1969. She was a Muslim, but he did not join the movement. They had one child, Sakina Ansari, but by 1972 the marriage broke up. Today, Wilson speaks with pride of his grown daughter.

Wilson did not actually see a play until 1976 when he saw Fugard's moving play about discrimination, *Sizwe Bansi is Dead*. In this same year he became interested in the idea of black music as a marketable commodity which was controlled by whites. While listening to a recording by Madame "Ma" Rainey, the idea came to him that through a play using her character he might explore the economic exploitation of early black performers. He began a play but did not complete it at the time. Later the completed *Ma*

Rainey's Black Bottom would provide his entry to the theatre world. Although he admired the aims and outlooks of many of his friends, and even admired people in the penitentiary because they had challenged the white establishment, he was not inclined toward agit-prop plays. Unlike many black playwrights, his own experience and his knowledge of the history of blacks in America has not resulted in bitter, vituperative dramas. Particularly in the sixties, some black playwrights were so militant against white culture that they alienated white audiences rather than bringing understanding to them. Critics have noted this difference, observing that Wilson movingly evokes the evolving psychic burden of slavery without laying on guilt or political harangues. Claude Purdy, who had started a black theatre group in St. Paul, encouraged Wilson in his first efforts at playwriting. He said of Wilson, "August came out of the '60s with a responsible attitude, eager to explore his community's culture and do something for his people" (S049). Wilson (A07) wrote that he came to manhood at a time when black Americans were pronouncing their social awareness, debating the character of their culture, and seeking ways to alter their relationship with society and that he felt it was a duty and a privilege to participate.

As director-in-residence at the Penumbra Theatre, Claude Purdy asked Wilson to write a play for the theatre. Wilson wrote a musical satire called *Black Bart and the Sacred Hills*. He traveled to Los Angeles with Purdy for a staged reading in 1978 then to St. Paul which he liked so much that he moved there. The 1982 production of the play was the first professional staging of his work. Like other earlier works, Wilson left it aside as he moved on with increasing strength as a writer. Another important result of Wilson's friendship with Purdy was his introduction to the art of Romare Bearden. Wilson has often called the painter Bearden an artistic mentor who gave a solidifying purpose to his writing.

One reason Wilson did not complete *Ma Rainey's Black Bottom* was his difficulty with characterization and dialogue. This changed as he learned to listen to his characters, particularly after moving to St. Paul which had a small black population. He had grown up in a neighborhood with 55,000 blacks and moved to a state with only 34,000 blacks. Away from his roots and the culture in which he grew up, he gained a new appreciation of the language he had heard all his life. He learned to "listen" to the voices of his past and create dialogue with reality, poetry, and dramatic quality. Wilson liked the city and through Purdy met Judy Oliver, a social worker whom he later married. He remained in St. Paul despite the connections he was soon to form with the Yale Repertory Theatre and Broadway.

In his early years in St. Paul, however, he had no certainty that he would be able to achieve success as a poet or in theatre, to which he had become increasingly attracted. In 1978 he was hired by the Science Museum to write short plays for the Children's Theatre. In this unlikely setting he wrote one-person shows about such characters as the Mayan Indian weaving woman who performed by a Mayan hut. Other characters included Margaret Mead, William Harvey, and a man who collected Indian artifacts with which he demonstrated how the Indians ground their corn, etc. In some of the playlets such as "How Spider Woman Taught the Navajo to Weave," mythic elements were present. Wilson noted the significance of these pieces in his development as a playwright, saying, "In working those out there was interest because you were doing different things. You were creating a character for a specific purpose, demonstrating the artifacts in the museum. Those were fun to write." (S088) However, in 1981 Wilson quit the Museum to work as a cook for a social service organization called the Little Brothers of the Poor. For three years he cooked half the day and wrote the other half.

In this period Wilson sent four scripts to the Eugene O'Neill Theater Center's Playwrights Conference in Connecticut: two film scripts and plays called *Fullerton Street* and *Jitney*. The competition was (and is) intense and the scripts were returned. Wilson submitted *Jitney* to the Minneapolis Playwrights' Center and was given a Jerome Fellowship which provided him about $200 a month. Perhaps even more importantly, he felt he had become a playwright. He walked into a room with sixteen other playwrights and he thought that he must be one, too. He found that a very important factor in his continuing efforts to succeed. In fact, he was on the verge of success with the play he was writing, *Ma Rainey's Black Bottom*. He sent that to the O'Neill Center in 1981 and it was accepted. Each year about fifteen plays were selected for staged readings out of approximately 1500 which were submitted. Artistic Director Lloyd Richards said that when he read the script the words leaped off the page and he recognized an authentic voice talking about real people and real situations.

In the summer of 1982 the play was given two staged readings by professional actors for audiences which included professional critics. Wilson traveled to Waterford, Connecticut, for the Conference and there he became acquainted with Richards. He was initially so in awe of him that he hardly spoke to him, but a relationship between the two swiftly developed in which Richards became a sort of surrogate father to Wilson and his chief advisor on playwriting. The two quickly moved into a working relationship which has lasted through the years based on Richards' intuitive response to the plays and Wilson's trust in his suggestions. Wilson has often said that Richards understands the overall arc of his work and has a keen sense of what should be cut and what should be left in the scripts. Richards, then Dean of the Yale School of Drama, directed *Ma Rainey's Black Bottom* at Yale Repertory Theatre and began a process which continued for the subsequent plays: a staged reading at the the Conference, production at Yale, then "production sharing" at regional theatres throughout the country, allowing Wilson the time to rewrite, cut, and polish before the production opens in New York. Wilson is thus often working on two or more plays at once as he does not like to have one play open until the next is completed.

When *Ma Rainey* opened in New York in 1984 it received the prestigious Drama Critics Circle Award. Although a few critics found the play lacking in plot, most greeted it enthusiastically, lifting Wilson into the category of major playwright seemingly overnight.

Wilson's next play, *Fences*, opened in New York in 1987 and garnered even more praise winning the Pulitzer Prize, the Tony Award for Best Play, and the Drama Critics Circle Award, as well as other prizes. It was the first play to capture all of the major awards in thirty years. Critics expressed the opinion that James Earl Jones was superb in the great role Wilson had created. By this time Wilson was pursuing what he has often described as a cycle of plays dealing with the "auto-biography" of blacks in America. He noted of the cycle that every event and character he put on the stage is made of himself and his experience. Each play is to treat one decade of the twentieth century with *Fences* representing the '50s. Although Wilson has little interest in films (in 1980 he saw his first film in twelve years), he sold the rights to Paramount as a vehicle for Eddie Murphy, who wanted to play the young son. Controversy arose when Wilson wanted to have a black director for the screenplay and the film has not been made. Many people have been critical of Wilson's stance and have suggested that if it is carried to a logical conclusion, only white men could direct plays and movies written by white men, Jewish women plays and movies written by Jewish women, etc. In 1997 this attitude about black directors for his work came under close questioning in connection with a speech he presented for the Theatre Communications Group.

It was estimated that Wilson earned more than a million dollars in the year following the success of *Fences*. However, the sudden prosperity made little difference to this child of the ghetto--he said he only needed money for beer and cigarettes and had not changed his apartment, car, or lifestyle. The many interviewers who now took an increasing interest in Wilson often noted his modesty, his quiet style, and his charm. He was enjoying living in St. Paul and being associated with the Penumbra Theatre. He was sometimes called "The Bard of St. Paul" and was a source of pride to the city as the only Minnesotan ever to win the Pulitzer Prize for playwriting. In 1987, Mayor George Latimer proclaimed May 27 August Wilson Day.

    Joe Turner's Come and Gone opened in New York in 1988 and Wilson found himself in the unusual position for any playwright, particularly a black one, of having two plays running on Broadway. Some critics felt this was his best play to date and it won the Drama Critics Circle Award. As with earlier plays, it introduced some outstanding black actors to audiences who went on to major careers and it has been performed widely in regional theatres. An interesting picture of the difficulties faced by a playwright in the contemporary American theatre is given by the events which occurred shortly after *Joe Turner's Come and Gone* opened. Despite the awards and rave reviews--perhaps even because of them--after less than a month there were not enough ticket sales to justify keeping the play running. It was supposed that many people did not hurry to see it because they assumed that it would naturally have a long run. The absence of a familiar star's name may also have been a problem. When the producer announced the play would close, Katherine Hepburn, Lou Gosset, Jr., and others rushed to see it and to encourage others to do so. Billy Dee Williams, then starring in *Fences*, gave a curtain speech urging people to enjoy a wonderful evening in the theatre by going to see *Joe Turner's Come and Gone*. As a result, the play did not close as announced. These events indicate the high esteem in which Wilson is held by the theatrical community.

    Wilson has stated that *Joe Turner's Come and Gone* is his favorite play of those he has written. He has often discussed the impetus to write it after seeing a painting by Romare Bearden called "Mill Hand's Lunch Bucket" which was the original title of the play. He was inspired by the prosaic subject matter of one man coming down the stairs of a boarding house reaching for his lunch bucket, while a woman with her purse is going out the door, and a child sits at a table drinking a glass of milk. The central figure who moved Wilson to wonder about his life was a man with a hat and coat sitting in a posture of abject defeat (S058).

A Bearden painting, "Piano Lesson," inspired his next play, too. He and Claude Purdy saw a Bearden exhibit and by the next day Wilson was enacting speeches he had in his head. With *The Piano Lesson,* Wilson provided Charles S. Dutton, who had played the dynamic trumpet player in *Ma Rainey*, a complex, exuberant role. The play again received high praise, with some dissenters, and won for Wilson his second Pulitzer Prize and all the major awards. With this string of successes, critics began to wonder if Wilson could keep it up and if, like so many other playwrights, he would defect to Hollywood. Wilson, however, is committed to theatre and pursued his career with a new play called *Two Trains Running.*

Again he provided stunning roles, especially for long-time actor Roscoe Lee Browne and Larry Fishburne (now Laurence) who won a Tony award as best actor. (Fishburne has since established a major career in films.) He was working on a new play set in a turpentine camp and he said he intended to complete one play to be performed as part of the arts festival in connection with the Olympics in Atlanta in 1996. Neither of these projects reached fulfillment, possibly because of a certain amount of upheaval in his life.

By the time *Two Trains Running* opened, a number of changes had occurred. Wilson and his wife divorced and he moved to Seattle. His situation regarding premieres of his plays changed when Lloyd Richards had to retire from Yale because there is a limit on the number of years a Dean can serve. Although he had expressed the view that antismokers were obnoxious and he did not intend to quit, Wilson did quit his four-pack-a-day cigarette habit cold turkey. Used to writing in such locations as a diner in New Haven and coffee shops in St. Paul, he now found himself in a new life, without a familiar locale in which to write. There was a gap between the appearance of his last play and the next, *Seven Guitars.*

When that opened in 1995, it was not at the Yale Repertory Theatre, but at the Goodman Theatre in Chicago, and Richards had to drop out of the production because of illness. The Chicago premiere received mixed reviews, with some critics noting that the usual process of "production sharing" and rewriting would undoubtedly improve the play. Happily Richards recovered and he and Wilson worked on the play as it moved from one non-profit theatre to another around the country. Wilson rewrote, adding characters and dropping characters, and this complicated the production and involved a number of cast changes.

The fine-tuning continued before *Seven Guitars* finally opened in New York in March 1996. The play opened to positive reviews with most critics praising the first act but finding the second weaker. One critic suggested that Wilson revise the second act further. With a strong ensemble cast the play was entertaining and moving, and continued to demonstrate Wilson's love for the blues. The setting was praised and many critics noted the flamboyant costumes by Constanza Romero, now Wilson's wife. Wilson's play won him his sixth Drama Critics Circle Award. The play was nominated for eight Tony Awards, but the only one which came its way was the Tony for best featured actor which went to Ruben Santiago-Hudson who played Canewell.

Shortly after the play opened, Wilson was honored at the William Inge Theatre Festival in Kansas. During the Tribute to August Wilson, he accepted the "William Inge Festival Award for Distinguished Achievement in the American Theatre." In June he delivered the keynote address to the Theatre Communications Group and as a result, his name was very much in the news. His speech decried the absence of regional professional black theatres, condemned the idea of colorblind casting, and blamed critics such as Brustein for many of the problems in contemporary theatre. Brustein and others responded with harsh comments for Wilson. Following a strong critical exchange in print, Wilson and Brustein agreed to meet in a so-called debate at Town Hall in New York in January 1997 with Anna Deavere Smith as moderator. During the meeting, Wilson was intense and showed none of his usual humor. The "debate" produced no change in either of the speakers despite efforts of the moderator to bring them together. Brustein said that he had discovered that Wilson was "a teddy bear" to which Wilson replied, "I may be personable, but I assure you I am a lion" (S215). The intense response to this meeting, both during the evening and in print later, brought out hostility toward both speakers. In particular, Wilson was called a separatist and criticized for not having done enough to help black theatres himself although his plays are frequently produced in white professional theatres throughout the country. He is philosophical about the response, since he feels that it is almost impossible to get even five people to agree about something, so that a theatre full of people are sure to disagree.

Following the production of Wilson's plays in New York, resident theatres began to produce his plays with great success, often in locations where there was a limited black audience and/or other plays by black playwrights had not drawn audiences. The Baltimore Center Stage recently presented *Two Trains Running* which was the biggest hit, by far, of the last several years. His plays have thus been important in increasing theatre attendance by members of the African American community, introducing white audiences to a wider range of works, and showing that the production of plays by black playwrights is financially viable. Writing in 1994, Andrew B. Harris (S127) observed, "Young and racially mixed audiences flock to see the latest August Wilson Play." Many regional theatres have produced all of Wilson's plays, and some actors travel around the country from one theatre to another appearing in his plays. Wilson likes to see his plays at different theatres with different casts. Jim Ponds, who has acted in all of Wilson's plays, said it is a great experience working with Wilson and in his plays, but noted that for some resident theatres there is still a special perception of the plays: they are usually produced in February, Black History Month, so the production of a Wilson play is a once-a-year event. There are some signs that this is changing, however, because of the popularity of the plays. The Penumbra Theatre (with resident black casts) says that Wilson's name sells season tickets and that the plays lend themselves to being done again, and certainly are worth doing again (S164). They opened their twentieth season with *Ma Rainey's Black Bottom* and closed with *Fences*.

In the relatively short time Wilson has been writing for the theatre he has created a body of work which transcends the usual commercial Broadway product, partly because of the scope of his intentions and partly because of the high rate of critical and popular success he has enjoyed. Compared to a playwright like Eugene O'Neill, his body of work is small. At this point there is no concensus regarding the relative merit or lasting quality of his plays. Yet, he is already one of the most honored playwrights in America. It was inevitable that his work would be compared to that of Eugene O'Neill as there are many similarities. In fact, Clive Barnes (R063) called his review of *Joe Turner's Come and Gone* "O'Neill in Blackface," noting similarities in technique and mood between the two playwrights. Reviewing *The Piano Lesson* in London, Michael Billington (R138) observed that in Wilson, as in O'Neill and Ibsen, the past constantly informs the present. Of course, Wilson is associated in critics' minds with O'Neill because his first opportunities were at the Eugene O'Neill Theatre Center. Just as O'Neill provided great acting opportunities for black actors including Charles Gilpin and Paul Robeson, so Wilson has provided great roles for black actors including James Earl Jones, Yaphet Kotto, Charles S. Dutton, Viola Davis, Michele Shay, Mary Alice, and Laurence Fishburne. Both playwrights won the Pulitzer Prize more than once. Like O'Neill, Wilson envisions a cycle of plays utilizing the history of America. Like O'Neill, Wilson writes about serious subjects, but mixes comedy and tragedy. But more important than these similarities is the shared viewpoint about the drive to write and the significance of the written plays.   As O'Neill wrote about matters which disturbed him emotionally, Wilson says he is writing about the "stuff that beats" in his head. Both playwrights wrote in order to create works of art, rather than for financial gain. Wilson continues his modest lifestyle, preferring a quiet, simple life: "Give me my books and records and I'm happy." (One change in his life in 1997 will be the birth of a child to Wilson and his wife Constanza Romero, a circumstance which fills him with happiness.)

The comparisons to O'Neill, however, have not been all favorable. Brustein (S105) wrote that premature praise was an obstacle O'Neill had to overcome and expressed the view that Wilson had been extravagently praised for his works and was reaching a dead end in his plays dealing with racism and black culture. Brustein and other critics have objected to Wilson's use of the supernatural in his plays, Brustein describing the ending of *The Piano Lesson* as ludicrous and an example of poor construction. Objecting to the the reverence accorded Wilson in America, Morley (R143) said that play was much too long and the ending was laughable. In his view, the British director was trying to "haul" Wilson into O'Neill's league. Weeks (S136), remarking that Wilson was the first major playwright since O'Neill to believe in spirits, questioned Wilson about his use of the supernatural. Wilson said that sort of folklore is a part of black culture which he experiences everywhere. He is unlikely to be affected by such comments, as he and Richards both rejected efforts to change the ending of *Fences* when the producer felt it was unrealistic.

It is also unlikely that Wilson will start to write short plays. He admits that he overwrites, but he feels that is better than underwriting. He says he doesn't mind cutting at all. In fact *Fences* initially ran four and one-half hours, then he cut an hour, and when it opened in New Haven it was two hours and ten minutes long. Wilson is going against the contemporary preference for shorter plays with less density of language and more visual elements. Earlier in the American theatre such writers as Robert Sherwood, Eugene O'Neill, S. N. Behrman and others often wrote long plays with a focus on language, not action, and audiences and critics readily accepted them. Now critics and audiences expect shorter plays, but many writers have observed, some rather tartly, that Wilson can get his long plays produced and that audiences enjoy them. (However, he is presently revising *Jitney* at the Crossroads Theatre in New Brunswick, New Jersey, where he is in residence. This is a play he wrote eighteen years ago which, in fact, runs only about two and a half hours. It will be presented at the Manhattan Theatre Club in the fall of 1997.)

Even the critics who find Wilson's plays long and talky generally agree, however, that they do work theatrically and create power and excitement on the stage. Critics have written repeatedly about the excitement and power of Wilson's plays, his epic vision, power, poetic sense, and orgiastic climaxes toward which the action builds. Barnes (R090) wrote, "His gift for the seat-edging theatrical and thrillingly, mysteriously dramatic has made him the most acclaimed playwright of his time." From his first play to his last, Wilson has evoked a strong response from audiences and critics in New York and in resident theatres.

At a time when many American playwrights write about transitory problems, Wilson seeks the great themes. He believes that the present generation of American playwrights has been spoiled by a childhood spent with television rather than literature. Making a distinction between the artist and the craftsman, he cast his lot with the former, aspiring to the highest art. However, he regards his own work with modesty. He says he reads the reviews and often learns from them. His intention to write a play for each decade of the century has captured the imagination of the public and the critics. The latter often refer to this cycle, expressing interest and enthusiasm for the idea. Wilson says it will be great to have completed it, but that he will not then have exhausted the material, and will begin all over again. In various interviews he has expressed annoyance that some white critics have suggested he has written enough about black people. In interviews he often speaks with determination about the mistreatment of blacks in society, yet, as critics have remarked, in his plays he has always been more sensitive to metaphors than manifestoes. Bigsby (S135) wrote in 1992, "There is anger in the plays but it never shapes itself into polemic." Wilson has often expressed the idea that he hopes to introduce white audiences to the differences in sensitivies between blacks and whites so that they may look at blacks differently after seeing his plays.

Wilson occupies an unusual position in American theatre. Although he feels very passionate about the historical treatment of blacks in American society, his characters break through the barriers of race and speak to both whites and blacks because they relate to archetypal themes and questions: What is true freedom? What is it to be a man or woman? How does a family relate? What is the nature of responsibility? What, ultimately, is the purpose of life and how does one find one's own song? In plays filled with poetic images, Wilson explores these questions. There is excitement about what he will write in the future and enthusiasm for what he has written in the past. Many critics have expressed the view that of the present-day writers Wilson is the one who will still be discussed in the years to come. They also point to his distinctive style which is not to be mistaken for any other. Many playwrights abandon the theatre for more lucrative and secure fields of writing, and many just burn out, so it is impossible to know if Wilson will fulfill his early promise, but his record so far is encouraging. He tells interviewers that the prizes he has won have given him the inner fuel to continue his work in the theatre. He has all the honors and awards on his wall and he is very proud of them, but prizes them chiefly as incentives to further work. He has already begun work on a play called *King Hedley II* which follows the lives of some of the characters in *Seven Guitars* and some of their offspring. The play will be set in the '80s and will explore the deterioration of a black family in a society in which there are guns and violence and an absence of parental control. As the century moves to a close, it will be interesting to see what forms and themes Wilson will explore in his plays about the late twentieth century. He believes strongly in the need for more opportunities for African American playwrights and intends to take an active part in organizing a conference for them in the South in 1998.

The Plays: Summaries and Critical Overviews

The following is a collection of summaries and overviews of Wilson's dramatic canon. The summaries provide descriptions of central characters and outlines of the significant events of the plays. Each critical overview includes sketches of the play's stage history, critical responses, and ensuing scholarly assessments where possible.

When referring to a critic/scholar in this section, citations have been keyed in parentheses to the numbers assigned to that writer's published assessment in the Secondary Bibliography section of this text, followed by a page number when relevant.

Fences (1985)

The Characters--TROY MAXSON: garbage collector, former baseball professional with the "colored league," has spent time in prison, a large man of fifty-three years; JIM BONO: long-time friend, also a garbage collector; ROSE: married to Troy, loving and patient, but strong-willed; LYONS: Troy's son by a former marriage, thirty-four years old, wants to be a musician; GABRIEL: seven years younger than Troy, injured in World War II, carries an old trumpet tied around his waist, believes himself to be the Archangel Gabriel; CORY: son of Rose and Troy, strong and athletic, seventeen years old; RAYNELL: first seen as a baby then as a pretty seven-year-old girl, she is Troy's daughter by another woman.

   Plot Summary--ACT I, Scene 1: On a Friday afternoon in 1957
Troy and Bono come into the front yard of Troy's home. They are coming
from work, drinking from a bottle, and talking about some trouble Troy has
with his employers. Bono thinks Troy is paying too much attention to
Alberta, a pretty young woman visiting the Taylors. Rose enters and they
change the subject to dinner and to sports. Troy is bitter because he could
not play on the white teams and he refuses to allow his son to pursue sports.
The others say things have changed, but Troy can't see that. He tells some
tall tales about wrestling with death and buying furniture from the devil.
Lyons enters wishing to borrow money as it is pay day. Troy remarks that is
the only day he does come to see him and criticises him for trying to be a
musician instead of getting a regular job. Lyons says he doesn't want to haul
trash. Finally, Troy gives Rose his salary and tells her to give Lyons ten
dollars. After he leaves Troy puts his arm around Rose and tells Bono that
he loves her so much that he will still be making love to her Monday
morning when it is time to go to work.

   ACT I, Scene 2: The next morning Rose is humming and hanging out
laundry. Troy comes out and they chat about playing the numbers. Troy is
angered to discover that Cory has gone away to practice football. Rose says
that Troy is in a bad humor because of what happened at work on Friday.
Gabriel enters, singing about the fruit he wants to sell from his basket. He
says Troy is mad at him because he has moved over to Miss Pearl's house
where he has his own room and his own key. Rose exits to make breakfast
and Gabriel, after saying he has been chasing hellhounds, exits singing
about the judgment day. Rose returns to say that Gabriel is not eating right
and should be taken care of. But Troy says nobody wants to be locked up.
He bitterly points out that the government gave Gabriel a "lousy three
thousand dollars" because he was wounded by the Japanese. He got the
money and bought their house intending it to be a home for Gabriel. In a
bad mood, he says he is going to the Taylors to listen to the ball game.

   ACT I, Scene 3: It is later in the day and Rose is telling Cory his father
is angry that he wasn't there to help him work on the fence he is building
around the yard. Cory responds that for the last few Saturdays Troy has not
worked on the fence, but spent his time at the Taylors. Cory wants to know
if Rose has told his father about the recruiter who wants him to play
football in college. When Rose is alone Troy sneaks into the yard, grabs her
from behind, tries to kiss her, and chases her around the yard. Remembering
Cory, he calls him out and criticizes him for not working. He says he won't
sign anything for the recruiter and that Cory better quit football and get his

job back at the A&P. Depressed, Cory asks why his father has never liked him. Troy tells him he has given him food and shelter and life and that "liking your black ass wasn't part of the bargain." Alone with Rose, Troy denies her claim that he was too old to play for the white teams and that he is jealous of Cory's chance to play football. He gives a vivid description of the bleakness of his existence and exits into the house.

ACT I, Scene 4: It is Friday afternoon and Cory is running out of the house to play football. Troy and Bono enter drinking and talking over Troy's victory in demanding to be allowed to be a driver of the garbage truck. He sings an old song about his dog Blue and tells Rose the good news. Lyons enters, surprisingly to pay back ten dollars. Gabriel enters, delighted to see Lyons, "the king of the jungle." Troy denies that he is angry at Gabriel for moving away and paying rent elsewhere. He tells Lyons that he has found out that Cory has lied about his job, and that he is playing ball. He reminisces about his life as one of eleven children with a hard father and how he left home and walked two hundred miles to Mobile. There he turned to robbery, killed a man, and was sent to prison. He says that when he got out he met Rose and dedicated himself to her and to playing baseball. After the others leave, Cory enters demanding to know why his father has told the recruiter not to come, thus ruining his only chance. He accuses Troy of being jealous because he had no chance. Troy tells him he has now made a mistake: he has one strike against him. Troy warns him not to strike out.

ACT II, Scene 1: It is the following morning and has begun with trouble. Gabriel has been arrested and Troy had to go to the judge and pay fifty dollars. He wants Cory to come help him work on the fence. Bono says he sees no use in building the fence, but Troy says Rose wants it. Bono suggests that Rose is trying to fence in Troy's love. He sees that Troy is involved with Alberta, the young visitor in the neighborhood. Troy admits that he is trying to work it all out. Alone with Rose he tells her with great difficulty that he is going to be the father of another woman's child. Gabriel enters and the conversation becomes confused, but Rose sends him in the house for some watermelon. She says she has given Troy everything she could for eighteen years and that Troy should have stayed in her bed. He answers that Alberta gave him something he never had before, but she counters that she also had desires and frustrations. As they quarrel, Cory interferes and hits Troy. He tells his son that he now has two strikes and again warns him not to strike out.

ACT II, Scene 2: Six months later Rose and Troy are in the yard, and Rose demands to know if he is coming home Friday after work. She tells him that Gabriel has been locked up and that she knows he signed the papers. As they argue, the telephone rings. Rose answers and returns with the news that Alberta has died giving birth to the baby. Troy insists that Rose leave him alone, and as he walks around the yard in a quiet rage, he vows to build a fence to keep out Mr. Death. He tells Mr. Death to come for him anytime and he will be ready for him.

ACT II, Scene 3: In this short scene Troy arrives holding his new-born daughter. Rose agrees to care for the baby, but tells him he is now a womanless man.

ACT II, Scene 4: Lyons enters the yard, telling Rose he has come to pay twenty dollars back to Troy. He talks to Cory about his graduation and the difficulty of finding a job, then leaves. When Troy arrives, Rose has little time for him as she is busy, as usual now, going to the church. She tells him his dinner is in the kitchen. Alone, he sits on the steps and sings his song about his old dog Blue. He is surprised to see Bono who never visits now that Troy is a driver and no longer works with him. But Bono can't stay and again he is alone singing and drinking from his bottle. When Cory demands room to go by, an altercation begins. Cory claims that Troy never gave him anything and picks up a bat to hit Troy. They struggle and Troy just stops himself from hitting Cory with the bat and orders him out. Alone again, he tells Mr. Death to come on anytime.

ACT II, Scene 5: It is now 1965, the morning of Troy's funeral. Raynell is in the yard when Cory arrives, but she doesn't know him. Rose comes out and tearfully welcomes him. She says that Lyons will be there, as he has been given time out of jail for the funeral, but she doesn't yet know if the authorities will let Gabriel out. Lyons arrives and tells Cory that he was put in jail for forging checks. Lyons fondly remembers Troy as a batter who could strike out three times and then hit a home run. Cory has no such fond memories and tells Rose he won't go to the funeral. She is sympathetic but says that he can't become a man by refusing to go to his father's funeral. She reminisces about her marriage and says that she should have insisted that Troy give her some room to live. However, she says that Raynell has renewed her life. Raynell and Cory become acquainted by singing Troy's song about old Blue, and he decides to go to the funeral. Gabriel arrives full of joy, ready to tell St. Peter to open the gates to receive Troy. In a dramatic scene he tries to play the trumpet, but fails. Nevertheless, he dances, sings a strange song, and suddenly the gates of heaven stand open for Troy.

   Critical Overview--*Fences* followed the pattern of the previous play with a staged reading, then the premiere at Yale Rep, but it then was performed at several other not-for-profit theatres before opening on Broadway. It opened 26 March 1987 at the 46th Street Theatre (P2. 2) and ran for 526 performances. When Wilson's second play opened in New York, the critics were looking forward to it because of the success of *Ma Rainey's Black Bottom* and an awareness of the progress of the play throughout the country. Critics were also aware of Wilson's intention to write a decade-by-decade cycle of plays and noted that this play covered the '50s. Again, there were many positive reviews praising both the play and the production. Barnes (R031), noting that Wilson's first play was flawed, called the new one the strongest and most passionate dramatic writing since Tennessee Williams, a pulsing play which not only moved him, but transfixed him. He said it is wrong to describe Wilson as a "black" playwright, because of his ability to tell a story in an engrossing, powerful way which has appeal regardless of race. As with the first play, Barnes and others praised the leading actor (James Earl Jones) above the others, but noted an excellent cast and production directed by Richards which could not be praised too highly. Beaufort (R032) concurred, calling the play a work of depth, eloquence, and power which added needed stature to the season. He, too, noted the universal quality of the play. Henry (R035) was one of many critics to describe the play as representative of the tragedy of a whole generation. He called the play a major step forward for Wilson and said the American stage had not heard such an impassioned and authentic voice since the emergence of Mamet. Kissel (R036) noted the continuing musical quality of the dialogue, and said Wilson was one of the few American playwrights who could be described as a poet. He noted that the play was long, but that it was a blockbuster--a major American play passionately performed. Both Wallach (R043) and Kroll (R038) praised the play and performance, but felt that it lacked the excitement and raw cutting edge of his first play. Still, like many critics, Kroll called Wilson a leading new voice in American theatre. Rich (R040) in another long, thoughtful review noted, too, that the play was less "hot" than the play set in the '20s. but suggested that it might have more appeal to those who found the earlier play plotless. He spoke in detail of the power of the play and the wonderful production. There was unanimity about the performances and great praise for Jones, but several critics found fault with the play. Lida (R039) said the other actors weren't given enough to do, that the last scene was dismal, and the plot turns melodramatic. Nevertheless, he felt the play was rewarding because of the language and Jones' performance. Watt (R044) said that like the first play, this was better in individual scenes than as a wholly shaped play. He felt the dialogue was rich, but that the play was conventional and too long. The *Nation* had a very harsh review. Disch (R033) complained that the play had been given too much hype in the press and that it was like a coronation for Wilson--he may have been suggesting that the critics were being politically correct. For him, the evening was like listening to some boring drunk. The negative critics were definitely in the minority as the play won all the major awards and Jones was a shoo-in for the Tony for best actor. *Fences* has been frequently performed in resident theatres with success, and is supposed to be made into a film.

Joe Turner's Come and Gone (1986)

The Characters--SETH HOLLY: set apart from the other characters by his stability, is in his fifties, born of free parents, owns a boarding house, is a skilled craftsman; BERTHA HOLLY: his wife, married for twenty-five years, five years younger than her husband, she runs the household and works around his seeming bad-temper; BYNUM WALKER: a conjure man who works with roots and spells, a controlled man in his sixties, he is seeking a "shiny man" who will tell him that his song has been accepted; RUTHERFORD SELIG: a white peddler about Seth's age, he is from a family which first brought slaves to America, then recaptured runaway slaves, and he now reunites separated black people; JEREMY FURLOW: a happy young man who plays the guitar, about twenty-five, he is still a country boy trying to find his way; HERALD LOOMIS: thirty-two years old, out of place in society because he was forced to work for Joe Turner for seven years, sometimes possessed, wears a long overcoat and hat in August; ZONIA: his daughter, eleven years old, tall and skinny; MATTIE CAMPBELL: twenty-five years old, pretty, but disappointed and unhappy, she is seeking love; REUBEN MERCER: a lonely neighbor boy; MOLLY CUNNINGHAM: about twenty-six, attractive and carefree, on the move; MARTHA PENTECOST: married to Loomis, about twenty-eight, attractive but conservatively dressed, a member of an Evangelist church.

Plot Summary--ACT I, Scene 1: It is morning in Seth's rooming house in Pittsburgh in 1911. He is complaining to Bertha about Bynum who is casting spells in his garden, about Jeremy, who has been arrested, about the number of "country niggers" who come North looking for work, and about his white employers who won't loan him money to set up a business making pots and pans. Bynum enters and they all eat breakfast, then Selig enters with sheet metal for Seth to use to make dustpans which he will sell. Bynum tells him about his experience finding his song in life and his search for the shiny man who has the Secret of Life. He has given Selig a dollar to find him. Selig exits with garden vegetables given him by Seth. Jeremy appears complaining that the police arrested him for nothing, gave him no food, and charged him a two dollar fine. As he eagerly eats breakfast, Herald Loomis makes a startling entrance, asking for a room for himself and his daughter while he looks for his missing wife. Seth agrees to let him stay, but after showing him the room says that something "ain't setting right" with him. He realizes that Martha Pentecost is Loomis' long lost wife by the resemblance between Zonia and her, but refuses to tell Loomis. Now Mattie Campbell enters, also looking for someone. She has heard that Bynum can cast a spell which will bring her lover back to her. Bynum warns her that he can bind people together, but that some people should not be bound together. Jeremy takes the opportunity to propose himself as her lover and they agree to meet at eight when he will try his luck in a guitar playing contest. The act ends in a scene in which Zonia and Reuben get to know each other.

ACT I, Scene 2: Another Saturday morning at breakfast with Seth now complaining about Loomis whom he has seen hanging around the church looking sneaky. He still refuses to reveal Martha's whereabouts to Loomis. Again Selig enters, pleased to have the dustpans Seth has made. Loomis asks him to find his wife and he talks about the difficulties of marriage and of being a people finder. He exits saying he will look for Martha, but Bertha warns that Selig only "finds" people he previously took away and that Loomis has wasted his dollar.

ACT I, Scene 3: The next day at breakfast Jeremy enters and says he wants to bring Mattie Campbell in to live with him, but Bynum warns him that he is only perceiving part of her identity as a woman and that he has much to learn. Molly Cunningham enters and breezily asks for a room, saying that she might occasionally have some company. As the scene ends, Jeremy, much taken with her, tells Bynum he is beginning to understand what he was talking about.

ACT I, Scene 4: It is later that evening after a fried chicken supper. Seth loudly says they are all going to "Juba" and Jeremy begins drumming on the table as the others move around the table in an improvised dance reminiscent of the ring shouts of African slaves, but mixing in references to the Holy Ghosts. As the dance works up to a frenzy, Herald Loomis enters and shouts at them to stop. He demands to know what is so holy about the Holy Ghost, and, with Bynum's prompting, he tells of a strange vision he has seen of bones rising out of water, then being washed ashore with flesh on them, but unable to move. In his frenzy he tries to stand, but his legs won't hold him up and he can only skitter wildly across the stage.

ACT II, Scene 1: Seth is again complaining about Loomis while eating breakfast, and indicates his intention to put him out. When Loomis enters he tries to get him to leave, but Loomis insists he has the right to stay until Saturday and angrily goes out the door. Molly offends Bynum by rejecting his work as spooky and he goes out to the back yard. Left alone, Molly and Mattie express their different views of life. Molly wants only pleasure, loves only her mama, and wants no children. Mattie is willing to work, but wants a man and children to love. Jeremy returns from work, having been fired because he refused to pay a white man a bribe. Alone with Molly, he proposes that they travel together, with him making money from his guitar playing and gambling. She finally agrees, but warns him that she needs more than a dollar a day and says, "Molly ain't going South."

ACT II, Scene 2: As Bynum and Seth play dominoes, Seth sings a song about Joe Turner, the man who caught blacks and forced them to work for him. Loomis enters and objects to the song, finally revealing that he was taken by Turner and thereby separated from his wife and child. He is lost and wandering in somebody else's world. Bynum says that Joe Turner wanted Loomis' song, but that Loomis still has his song and must remember how to sing it. Loomis responds that he recognizes Bynum as "one of them bones people."

ACT II, Scene 3: Bynum is advising Mattie at breakfast, but Bertha tells him to leave Mattie alone. She advises the young woman to forget Jeremy (who has run off with Molly) and be glad to get rid of him. Mattie's time is coming, she says. Seth reminds Loomis that he must leave soon. Left alone with Mattie, Loomis says he thinks she is attracted to him as he is to her. But when he moves close to touch her, he admits that despite his need for her, he has forgotten how to touch.

ACT TWO, Scene 4: Reuben and Zonia are in the back yard talking about friendship, ghosts, and love. Reuben kisses Zonia and tells her that when they are grown he will marry her.

ACT TWO, Scene 5: Saturday has arrived and Loomis waits with Zonia for Selig's arrival. But Loomis is prepared to go to another city and continue the search for his wife. He heads for the door with Zonia, ready to move on. When Mattie gives Zonia a ribbon, he stops to say that a man looking for a woman would be lucky to find her. Bertha advises Mattie that all Loomis needs to straighten out is love in one hand and laughter in the other. Seth enters to say that Loomis, looking sneaky, is standing on the corner watching the house. Martha Pentecost enters eager to find her child and husband. Selig has found her and brought her back. When Loomis enters he accuses Martha of having deserted him, but she responds that she was put off their farm and had been searching for him and Zonia. But she killed her love for him because she believed he was dead. Now Loomis gives Zonia to her mama, but before he leaves breaks into a bitter attack about people, including Joe Turner, wanting to bind him. Bynum says he only bound the daughter to the mother. Martha tells him to put away the knife he has pulled and try to find Jesus. Loomis denounces Jesus as a great big old white man with a grin. In a series of dramatic speeches he declares that he doesn't need Jesus or anyone to bleed for him. He slashes his chest and rubs blood on his face. Freed from his past, he has found his song and exits. Mattie rushes out after him, and Bynum realizes that he has found his shiny man.

Critical Overview--With his third play to be presented in New York, Wilson was perceived as a major playwright who had achieved a permanent place in the American theatre and whose continuing cycle of black history was an important project. The play followed the same pattern as *Fences* allowing Wilson the opportunity to rewrite and cut as the play progressed throughout the country. *Joe Turner's Come and Gone* opened in New York at the Ethel Barrymore Theatre on 26 March 1988 (P4.3) and ran for 105 performances. As usual, the acting was praised with particular attention to the major role played by a man, this time actor Delroy Lindo. Nevertheless, it seemed that the absence of an established major star like James Earl Jones, resulted in a shorter run. At the same time there was increasing criticism, especially regarding structure and length. Nevertheless, most reviews were positive in some way. Playing off the title of the new work, Kroll (R066) headed the review "August Wilson's Come to Stay." He called the story irresistible and said that director Richards had mined all the sweetness, humor, and sense of tragedy and triumph in the play which was performed by actors rising to lyric heights. Barnes (R063) spoke of Wilson's theatrical genius and approved the slowly building structure of the play, the comedy, the universality of the theme, the black idiom, and the mixture of naturalism and symbolism, all beautifully acted and directed. Oliver (R067) had seen the play as a staged reading and noted some shifts in emphasis. She praised the play and the production, but noted (not disparagingly) that it was the "most remote and dispersed of all Mr. Wilson's plays." In a very short review Cohen (R064) praised everything, saying Wilson was at the crest of his powers and that the play was as evocative as *Fences* but more original. Winer (R072) noted steady improvement in Wilson's technique, calling the play more consistent than his first and less melodramatic than his second. She responded fully to the "strangeness and wonder" of the play, the performances, the characters' stories, and the stunning scene of the Juba. She noted, however, that some viewers might prefer *Fences* because of the big star role and the focus on a single family story. Watt (R070) wrote a short, wholly positive review noting the epic vision, poetic sense, and orgiastic climax. Wilson (R071) compared it to another recent opening, pondering the elements which made *Joe Turner's Come and Gone* a Broadway success while the other was not. He noted the importance of Wilson's rewriting, saying the play had been tightened since he saw it at Arena Stage in Washington. He praised Wilson's scope, his development of the action and theme, the volcanic eruption of the final scene, and concluded that he is an exceptional dramatist on several levels. Kissel (R065), while responding positively to the play, noted that it was by design less "jazzy" than *Ma Rainey's Black Bottom* and that a little more syncopation might have improved it. Rich (R068) wrote another long review, saying the play may be Wilson's most profound and theatrically adventurous, a play of "true mystery and high drama." Nevertheless, he concluded his detailed analysis of what he found to be a fascinating play by saying that the first act was too long, that the characterization of the children was weak, and Richards should have been more tough-minded in the process of refining the play. A very negative view of the play was expressed by Stearns (R069) who said the play just seemed to start over and over, with little action and nothing but scenes with people yelling at each other. He found the cast "so-so" on the whole and felt that the play would be seen by fans of *Fences* but that others should wait for something more lucid. Again, the negative comments were in the minority and Wilson's play won the New York Drama Critics Circle Award. Some critics gave more attention to his life and career because of his increasing importance, some noted productions of his other plays in regional theatres, and most noted that he now had two plays running on Broadway, an almost unheard of feat, particularly for a black playwright. Wilson has called this play his favorite and it, too, has joined the Wilson plays in production at resident theatres.

Ma Rainey's Black Bottom (1984)

The Characters--STURDYVANT: produces phonograph recordings, insensitive to black performers, aggressive; IRVIN: Ma Rainey's manager; tall, fleshy, proud of handling blacks; CUTLER: mid-fifties, leader of the band, plays guitar and trombone, sensible; TOLEDO: mid-fifties, the only one of the three who can read, but misapplies knowledge, plays piano; SLOW DRAG: mid-fifties, plays bass, bored by life, large, with a wicked smile he appears slow, but is intelligent; LEVEE: early thirties, bright, intelligent, flamboyant, ambitious, plays trumpet; MA RAINEY: short, heavy woman, wears fur coat and hat, fancy dress and jewelry, famous singer, but embittered by life; DUSSIE MAE: a sensual young woman in a tight yellow dress and fur jacket; SYLVESTER: Ma's nephew, a large country boy who stutters; POLICEMAN: works in Chicago, intends to arrest Ma Rainey.

Plot Summary--ACT I: In Chicago 1927 Irvin and Sturdyvant set up equipment in a recording studio as they await the arrival of Ma Rainey. Sturdyvant warns Irvin that he will not tolerate the high-handed behavior Ma exhibited in the last session, but Irvin says he will handle her. Three of the band arrive, well-dressed and apparently successful, but to Irvin's distress neither Ma nor the trumpeter, Levee, are with them. He takes Cutler, Slow Drag, and Toledo to the section of the stage which represents the band room and tells them to rehearse. Slow Drag says that Levee has gone out to buy some fancy shoes with money he won from Cutler shooting craps. Levee wants to impress a gal Ma Rainey had in the club the night before. When Levee arrives they kid him for spending a week's wages for shoes. He doesn't want to rehearse because the music is old-fashioned jug band music. He plans to get his own band and is writing songs to sell to Mr. Sturdyvant. As the men argue, Toledo bets Levee that he can't even spell music and, in fact, Levee spells it "M-U-S-I-K." Waiting for Ma to arrive, they continue arguing and telling stories. They point out that Levee is continually complaining and Levee does complain, particularly, that they want to rehearse an old version of a song, when he has written a new introduction. Finally, they begin to rehearse, with Slow Drag singing Ma's part. Irvin appears to ask about Ma and to confirm that they will use

Levee's version. When he leaves, Toledo points out that blacks can never fulfill themselves as long as they allow the white man to make all the decisions.

The lights come up in the studio where Sturdyvant impatiently attacks Irvin because Ma has not arrived. At last she arrives, accompanied by Dussie Mae, Sylvester, and a policeman. The conversation is confused and angry, but it becomes clear that Sylvester was driving her new car and ran into someone. When a cab driver refused to take blacks in his cab there was a fight and a policeman took them into custody. Irvin takes the policeman aside, slides money into his hand, and the policeman says it will be all right and exits. As Ma makes various complaints, Irvin tells Toledo to take some sandwiches down to the boys and then they will make the recording. The lights again go up on the band room and they continue to argue, eat the sandwiches, and express their conflicting views about life. They begin to rehearse and the lights go down on them and up on the studio where Ma tells Bessie Mae all the nice things she will buy for her. The sound of the band is heard as Irvin enters to say Ma's car is all right. He says they decided to use Levee's new introduction to the song, but Ma angrily says that she has decided to use the old one with Sylvester introducing her. They go down to the band room and she announces her choice, prompting Levee to contradict her, but she warns him that she makes the decisions. When they rehearse, Sylvester stutters so much that it seems hopeless. Levee tries to impress Sturdyvant by singing a song he has written, but later reveals his deep hatred for white men when the others kid him. The act ends as he tells them how his mother was raped by white men and that his father subsequently killed some of them, before he was lynched. After a pause, Slow Drag sings the old song, "If I had my way, I would tear this old building down."

ACT II: As the lights come up in the studio, Levee is flirting with Ma's gal, Dussie Mae, and it is clear that is the reason Ma is against him. Irvin wants them to record, but Ma demands that he bring her a Coke, then sends everyone but Cutler out to buy her a Coke. Ma tells Cutler that Levee is to be replaced. She bitterly complains that the white men like Irvin only want to make money out of her. The lights come up on the studio where Toledo reads a paper and Levee sings his song. When Dussie Mae enters, Levee kisses her and brags about his future and his sexual abilities. Finally Ma's Coke arrives and the session resumes. They try to record the "Black Bottom," but Sylvester continues to stutter. At last he does the introduction and the song is successfully completed. To everyone's dismay, the song was not recorded because someone, possibly Levee, kicked a plug out. Ma threatens to leave, but Irvin begs for fifteen minutes to fix things. The band goes to the band room where Levee is warned that he better leave Dussie Mae alone. The musicians' frustrations and conflicting beliefs are revealed in their continuing argument which rises to a climax when Levee mocks Cutler's God, saying God hates blacks. When Cutler attacks him, Levee pulls a knife and circles him in a frenzied manner, mocking Jesus as the lights fade to black. The lights come up in the studio as the last song is successfully recorded. Everyone is pleased with the session, but Ma criticizes Levee for improvising and fires him. She demands payment for Sylvester, gets it, and leaves with Dussie Mae and Sylvester. In the band room the men wait for their pay. Sturdyvant enters with the money, telling Levee his songs are no good and he will only give him five dollars for each. Shattered, Levee realizes he will not be able to record them as he had been promised. As the band prepares to leave, Toledo accidentally steps on Levee's shoe. In an explosion of fury, Levee stabs Toledo. Horrified by what he has done, he tries to pick him up, but Toledo is dead. Cutler calls for the white man to settle things as Levee painfully plays a muted trumpet.

Critical Overview---*Ma Rainey's Black Bottom* opened in New York at the Cort Theatre on 11 October 1984 (P5.2) following staged readings at the O'Neill Center and a premiere at Yale Repertory in New Haven. It ran for 275 performances and has since been performed at most resident theatres throughout the country. The first of Wilson's plays to receive a professional production in New York created a great stir. Most of the critical response was positive and many critics were fairly overwhelmed because Wilson was a new voice. Some critics had an idea of the impact of the play because they had seen it at the O'Neill Center or had heard reports of the production at Yale. Beaufort (R002) praised all aspects of the play and production, saying the play was filled with deep insights and humor. He said that Wilson's examination of racism in America was superbly portrayed. Kroll (R005) noted the significant subject matter and the fact that the play was at first comic but took an explosive turn. Like most of the critics, he felt that Dutton was astonishing as Levee. Frank Rich (R008) was profoundly impressed by the production and the play. He wrote a long review discussing it as an important work which presented part of the history of black America in a startling and theatrical play. He analyzed what would come to be standard in reviews of Wilson's plays: the importance of music and the use of long speeches which were like musical solos. He also noted the effective mixture of comedy with harrowing material which is based on suffering, and results in a fine work of art. Kissell (R004) was equally positive, calling it a play of great power and saying that Wilson wrote it with grace and sensitivity. He praised all aspects of the production. Like most critics, he singled out Dutton and praised his "shattering performance." He praised the dialogue in the play, noting that in contrast to some black playwrights, Wilson avoided jargon and had a fresh quality. The review in *Jet* (R006) praised the play as "bold, Black, and bluesy." The reviewer focused on the subject matter of the exploitation of black musicians by white record executives, the efforts of some blacks to make it in a white man's world, and the black on black hatred which was a frequent result. As with most of the critics, the reviewer praised all of the cast, but gave highest praise to Dutton. The reviewer ended on a note of pleasure because critics everywhere were praising Wilson as a major new voice in theatre. He hoped for a long run since a black playwright on Broadway is a rarity. Siegel (R009) was almost entirely positive, praising the dialogue which was musical and "in perfect pitch." He called the play "fireworks," but noted that it had some flaws. His chief objection was that the play shifted too swiftly, and jarringly, from comedy to a serious and startling conclusion. But several critics were less impressed with the total quality of the play, even though they found it exciting and interesting. Barnes (R001) was impressed by the central struggle depicted by Wilson, which he said focused on the musicians, not Ma Rainey. He praised the production and noted that individual scenes worked well, but that the play as a whole was never really there--nothing much happened. He also felt that the ending was abrupt and not adequately prepared for. Watt (R012) was more positive, calling it a superb production in all ways and describing Dutton as magnificent. But he felt, too, that it was more of a slice of life than a play, that Wilson had a tendency toward wordiness, and that there were some dull moments. Nevertheless, his review had a positive quality and he said the play was entertaining most of the time. Wilson (R013) had about the same response, praising the production, calling the evening interesting and saying the first rate cast and Richard's direction made up for shortcomings in the play. There was a lack of structure--the play consisted of pleasing banter and atmosphere, but the audience was waiting for something more. He also wished there had been a greater use of music. The only major strongly negative review came from John Simon (R100), noted for his acerbic responses to plays. He felt Wilson had promise but didn't deliver a real drama. All in all, it was a very impressive debut with little negative response. Wilson was, in fact, praised so highly that there was anticipation that he might win the major awards for the year. After the opening, Mitgang (S016) wrote a piece about Wilson, based on an interview for the *New York Times* saying that his first New York production was a powerful play which was reawakening audiences to "the wonder and dimensions of drama." He noted that Wilson had only a ninth grade education but that Lloyd Richards felt Wilson was a major American playwright on the basis of *Ma Rainey's Black Bottom*. This view was validated when Wilson was given a Tony nomination and won the New York Drama Critics Circle Award for the best play. Continuing productions of the play in resident theatres draw positive reviews and indicate that the play has wide appeal.

The Piano Lesson (1990)

The Characters--DOAKER: railroad cook aged forty-seven, has retired from the world; BOY WILLIE: thirty, boyish, talkative, brash man from the South; LYMON: his friend, also from the South, twenty-nine, straightforward, but quiet; BERNIECE: sister of Boy Willie, thirty-five, in mourning for her husband; MARETHA: her pretty daughter, eleven; AVERY: thirty-eight, ambitious convert to city life, wants to found a church and marry Berniece; WINING BOY: uncle to Berniece and Boy Willie, brother of Doaker, former jazz pianist, likes to drink; GRACE: pretty girl, attractive to Lymon who meets her in a saloon.

Plot Summary--ACT 1, Scene 1: Boy Willie noisily enters his Uncle Doaker's house in Pittsburgh in 1936, shouting for his uncle and sister. He has driven from the South with a load of watermelons along with his friend Lymon. The two of them want a drink and say that they are celebrating the death of a man named Sutter, whom they claim was drowned in his well by the "The Ghosts of the Yellow Dog." Berniece enters, angry about their noise and eager to have Boy Willie leave. He says he will go when he has sold the watermelons as well as the family piano so that he can buy Sutter's land to farm. Berniece has not played the piano for years, but she will not part with it. After she goes upstairs, she screams and returns saying she has seen Sutter's ghost. She leaves vowing never sell the piano, but Boy Willie tells Doaker that if he has to, he will cut it in half and sell his part.

ACT I, Scene 2: Wining Boy has unexpectedly appeared and sits drinking and talking about the Ghosts of the Yellow Dog and family affairs with Doaker. They both feel Berniece should forget her dead husband and grab a handful of life before it is too late. When Boy Willie and Lymon enter, they ask Wining Boy if it is true that he has gone where the train tracks of the Yellow Dog cross those of the Southern Cross and spoken to the Ghosts. He tells of his strange experience and says it changed his life. Boy Willie says he has the name of a white man who will buy the piano. They all drink some whiskey and Lymon and Boy Willie tell of how they ended up in the Parchman Farm penitentiary for stealing wood. Lymon says he wants to remain in the North, but Boy Willie says he will return to the South and get his farm. Wining Boy says he will go with him, but warns that Boy Willie can't succeed against the white man. They all sing a song and then Doaker explains the history of the piano. It was carved with pictures of their family by his grandfather, then a slave in the Sutter family. Later, the piano was stolen by his brother, who was then burned to death in a railroad car on the Yellow Dog line by white men seeking revenge. These men have died mysteriously since. Berniece enters and is pleased to see Wining Boy, but eager to have Boy Willie gone. When he and Lymon attempt to move the piano, the sound of Sutter's ghost is heard. Again, Berniece tells Boy Willie she will not sell the piano which is steeped in their family's blood. The act rises to a climax as she attacks him, saying her husband died because Boy Willie got him involved in stealing wood and the sheriff shot him.

ACT II, Scene 1: Doaker is singing and preparing to leave for work on the railroad when Wining Boy enters with a silk suit he has unsuccessfully tried to pawn. Doaker gives him an update on family affairs saying Berniece is at work, Boy Willie and Lymon are out selling watermelons, and that he saw Sutter's ghost before Berniece did, but kept it quiet. Boy Willie and Lymon enter excitedly, telling of their success selling watermelons to white people. Wining Boy seizes the opportunity to sell Lymon his suit, claiming it is magic and will cause the women to fall for him. Boy Willie and Lymon exit, Wining Boy following so he can watch the women fall out of their windows when they see Lymon.

ACT II, Scene 2: Berniece is heating water on the stove to take a bath. Avery appears and talks to her about his church and pleads with her to marry him. She says she isn't ready to marry anyone. It is apparent she is distressed because she believes Boy Willie pushed Sutter in the well and that is why Sutter's ghost is in the house. She asks Avery to bless the house and drive the ghost away, which he reluctantly promises to do as he leaves.

ACT II, Scene 3: Boy Willie enters the dark house with Grace and tries to get her onto the couch with him, but they knock over a lamp and waken Berniece. She says she doesn't allow that kind of stuff in her house and tells Boy Willie to take "his company" away. As she makes some tea, Lymon appears, frustrated in his search for a woman. They talk about his future and he offers Berniece a bottle of perfume. Putting some behind her ears, he says she smells good, then kisses her. At first unresponsive, she finally returns his kiss then moves to go upstairs. Lymon strokes his suit, believing that it is indeed magic.

ACT II, Scene 4: As Lymon sleeps on the couch, Boy Willie enters excitedly saying he wants to move the piano because he has got a good price for it from the white man. Doaker enters and demands that they leave the piano alone until Berniece returns from work. They exit, but Boy Willie proclaims that he will be back with a rope and materials to move the heavy piano.

ACT II, Scene 5: As the lights come up Boy Willie is screwing casters on a plank and telling Maretha the history of the piano and the Ghosts of the Yellow Dog. Berniece enters and tells Maretha that she will straighten her hair, but Maretha is frightened to go upstairs to get the comb and the grease. Boy Willie goes with her saying he will "whup" Sutter's ghost if it exists. When they return Berniece threatens Boy Willie, but he says he isn't afraid of death and explains his philosopy of life and his belief in his future. He blames Berniece for teaching Maretha that she is at the bottom and claims that he is at the top. Avery arrives ready to get rid of Sutter's ghost, then Lymon enters with rope to move the piano. He has been drinking with Grace and is in a hurry to rejoin her. As they work on the piano, Berniece appears with a gun and the argument continues. Wining Boy enters drunk and begins to play the piano and sing. The argument over the piano resumes and Grace enters, tired of waiting for Lymon. When the presence of Sutter's ghost is again felt, she hurriedly leaves, followed by Lymon. Berniece asks Avery to bless the house and he prays and sprinkles water on the piano. Boy Willie takes water from the kitchen and throws it all over, telling Sutter to "get his ass out of the house." Working himself into a frenzy, he challenges Sutter and runs up the stairs. Avery says he can do nothing as Boy Willie engages in a life and death battle with Sutter, so Berniece seats herself at the piano and passionately sings, calling on her dead relatives for help. As calm takes over the house, Boy Willie enters and tells Wining Boy they need to go catch the train. He exits, telling Berniece she must play the piano in the future or else he and Sutter may both return.

Critical Overview--_The Piano Lesson_ followed the now familiar pattern of the staged reading, the opening in New Haven, work on the play through presentations in several cities, and a successful opening in New York. It opened on 9 January 1988 at the Walter Kerr Theatre (P7.3) and ran for 329 performances. With Wilson's new play there was enthusiastic response on the part of most critics, but some negative attitudes suggested earlier were carried to the point of large-scale criticism of his technique. The highly positive tone of most critics was previewed before the play opened in New York with the announcement that Wilson had been awarded his second Pulitzer Prize. It subsequently won several other awards establishing Wilson firmly as a major American playwright.With this play, more than ever, critics praised Wilson's ability with language and his qualities as a story-teller. Barnes (R090) set the general note of critical response, calling the play a wonderful Pulitzer Prize winner and Wilson the most acclaimed playwright of his time. Like many critics before and later he praised Wilson's ability to write comedy. Again, Richards was praised for directing the best ensemble playing on Broadway. Rich (R096) again wrote a long review noting that Wilson writes his own style, not trying to accomodate himself toward the establishment. He called the play musical throughout its bubbling three hours and praised the miraculous voice Wilson had given the black characters. These were wondrously performed and, in particular, Dutton was a character on fire. Nevertheless, Rich noted dead ends and repetition in the second act. Beaufort (R091), in contrast, felt that the digressions are really part of the fabric of the play which was theatrically superb, reconfirming Wilson's major status as a playwright. Like almost all of the critics he praised Dutton's performance. Kissel (R092) felt that the digressions didn't advance the central story but were fascinating because of Wilson's ability with language and, further, felt the play was important because it might help move the American theatre out of the rut of naturalism. Winer (R104) continued as a major Wilson fan, calling the play a lovely tragi-comedy, haunting as well as haunted. But she and many other critics felt the ending was unsatisfactory. Spillane (R097) praised all other aspects but felt that Wilson had not improved the ending, since she had seen the play in New Haven. Edwin Wilson (R103) agreed and, like many others, felt the play was too long. Two negative reviews appeared in the _New Yorker_ and _USA Today_. Kramer (R094) found the play too long, the ending mystical and melodramatic, and the conclusion unclear. She found Dutton tiresome. Stearns (R098) said some of the individual scenes were among the most compelling Wilson had written, but that Dutton was obnoxious and he did not feel the play would please audiences because it was easy to respect, but not to enjoy. Brustein (S105) who had not cared for Wilson's earlier plays, but had refrained from reviewing them, attacked the play as long and poorly written, and totally lacking in poetry. He further stated that the presence of a ghost in a realistic play showed that the playwright had not mastered his material. Writing in 1994, Harris (S162) praised the play and said the audience didn't need to believe in spiritual possession to understand that a "brother and sister can be haunted by a spirit that appears to emanate from the ancestral piano" (127). The play received more hostile criticism than any earlier play, but in addition to the Pulitzer Prize, won the New York Drama Critics Circle Award, a Tony nomination, the award from American Theatre Critics for the Outstanding Play, and the Drama Desk Award. Again, the Wilson play has found success in the many resident theatres, some of which have by now performed all of his plays.

Seven Guitars (1996)

The Characters--VERA: a woman who loved Floyd and suffered when he left her for another woman, twenty-seven years old; LOUISE: a mature woman whose husband left her only his gun; loves to smoke Old Golds; RED CARTER: a drummer who plays with Floyd; CANEWELL: a harmonica player who plays with Floyd, attracted to Vera; HEDLEY: a fifty-nine year old mystic who earns a living by killing and cooking chickens to make sandwiches; FLOYD (SCHOOLBOY) BARTON: ambitious guitar player who has been in jail for ninety days, thirty-five years old; RUBY: Louise's twenty-five year old niece, sexy and well-dressed.

Plot Summary--ACT I, Scene 1: In Pittsburgh in 1948 the friends of Floyd Barton are in the back yard of a tenement, drinking and talking about Floyd and his funeral. Floyd had returned to Pittsburgh after being in jail and was about to go to Chicago to follow upon the success of a hit record he had made earlier. They are eating and drinking and talking about the past. Vera and Canewell say that they saw angels taking him up to heaven, but Red says he always swore Floyd would go straight to hell. Red asks Vera to put on Floyd's recording and soon "That's All Right" is heard. After a moment of silent reverie, Red says, "Floyd 'Schoolboy' Barton."

ACT I, Scene 2: The play reverts to the time of Floyd's return. He is dancing with Vera in the yard in back of the tenement house. He makes sexual advances which she rejects. He tries to convince her that he loves and needs her, but she speaks bitterly of how he left her and the lonely nights she spent. He says that he shouldn't have left her for another woman, but that he thought she believed in him more than Vera. Now he says he is in demand, the people in Chicago want him to make another record and are addressing him as Mister. He is bitter about the past because he was jailed for "worthlessness" but he looks forward to a bright future. He has come to get Vera to go with him to Chicago, get his guitar out of hock, and also to get his two sidemen, Red and Canewell. Louise enters and announces that her young niece will be arriving because of "man trouble" down in Alabama. When she leaves Floyd again urges Vera to make love with him. She goes into her apartment and he follows as the sound of his recording swells.

ACT I, Scene 3: Hedley enters singing a song about Buddy Bolden and prepares to kill and cook his chickens. Hedley speaks of George Butler who has died and also says he knocked on Louise's door the night before. She says the gun her man left her is all the man she needs. She urges Hedley to go to the sanitarium which is now "letting in the colored people" so he will not die of T.B. like George Butler. Canewell enters with a Golden Seal plant for Vera. He and Hedley immediately start to argue about the Bible and salvation. He says the neighbors have gone next door to tell Mrs. Tillery to get rid of her rooster which wakes them up early in the morning. He wants to see Floyd and calls him to the window. But when Floyd asks him to go to Chicago, he refuses because he was arrested there. When Floyd sees Hedley he sings the song about Buddy Bolden and engages in repartee with him about the fact that Hedley expects to see the ghost of Bolden who will give him some money. Vera enters and Canewell gives her the Golden Seal plant which will cure any ill health. They plant it in the yard. As Floyd leaves with Canewell to go to the pawnshop, Vera tells him to bring back some groceries and pay the light bill. Floyd says he is taking his old guitar to the pawnshop, then going out to see his mother's grave. He reminds Hedley that Joe Louis is fighting that night.

ACT I, Scene 4: Louise is telling Vera about her niece with a "fast little behind." Floyd and Canewell enter and Floyd furiously says the people refused to give him his pay for his work in prison because he didn't have the right papers. Red enters and when asked says he will not go to Chicago with Floyd, but changes his mind when Floyd describes the pretty women there. Vera and Louise exit to cook greens. Hedley enters and the talk turns to God, but Floyd disparages God and says he doesn't want to hear about the Bible. The talk turns to getting arrested and the use of weapons. Floyd shows his .38, Red his .32, but Canewell prefers a pocket knife. The talk has an ominous edge, increased by Hedley's appearance with a large butcher knife. The talk turns to music and they play and sing, and as Floyd's thoughts turn to his mother he sings the "Lord's Prayer." Vera puts the radio in the window and says the fight is starting.

ACT I, Scene 5: All the characters are in the back yard listening to the fight. When Joe Louis wins they shout and dance. Red says he will teach Vera a dance called "Jump Back." It is very sensual and Floyd's jealousy leads to a confrontation between the two men and Floyd pulls out his .38. Just then Ruby enters carrying her suitcase. All of the men find her attractive and she seems to lead them on. She exits and the others play cards. As they play and chat about Mother's Day, they are annoyed by the rooster next door and Floyd throws a stone. Hedley exits and reenters in a deranged fashion carrying the rooster which he kills with his knife. He says the rooster was "too good live for your black asses," sprinkles the blood in a circle and predicts that they will soon be dead. Everyone is stunned and the scene ends.

ACT II, Scene 1:   Hedley is alone onstage preparing his sandwiches and eggs. As Floyd's record plays on a radio in the house he sings his usual song about Buddy Bolden. Ruby enters and asks for one of his eggs. She wonders why he killed the rooster senselessly as one her boyfriends senselessly killed the other. He explains his obsession with Buddy Bolden to her. His father was a musician who loved Buddy Bolden more than his family and named his Hedley "King" after him. Hedley once killed a black man because he would not admit that Hedley was King. Hedley wants to be a big man, but he would be happy to have a son who would be great like Marcus Garvey. He tells Ruby he wants to be the father of a messiah with her, but she is not interested. When Floyd arrives to get his old guitar he sees Ruby and says he will take her around and show her Pittsburgh. Hedley is angry and jealous, reminding Floyd that he should be trying to get his guitar out of hock. Floyd's bad luck continues, though, and he says he cannot get his guitar because the ticket expired while he was in jail. Hedley busies himself and sings about Buddy Bolden, prompting Floyd to say he needs money so badly that he would be glad to have Buddy

Bolden or Brer Rabbit give it to him. Hedley says he has waited many years since his dream that his father would send Buddy Bolden with money for him. Once Bolden came, but only gave him ashes. As Floyd leaves with Ruby he assures Hedley he will get the money. Hedley ominously warns Floyd that because he is a king the white people have a plan against him and that he should be careful.

ACT II, Scene 2: Vera and Louise are in the yard, talking as Vera makes paper flowers for Mother's Day. Louise is ready for Ruby to take her fast little behind away and get a job. Ruby enters and casually reveals that she is pregnant and doesn't know which of her lovers is the father. Canewell and Floyd enter excitedly telling the news that they will play at the Blue Goose for the Mother's Day Dance and that Mr. T.L. Hall has arranged a recording date in Chicago. Floyd has given all his money to the gravestone man to ready a marker for his mother's grave. In the midst of the excitement, Hedley enters furiously, flings his baskets around and throws a crumpled letter down in front of Louise. He shouts about a plot against the black man and says he won't go anywhere. He stomps on the letter and exits. Louise explains that she called the board of health to say Hedley needed to go to the sanitarium for his T.B. The characters are divided in their reaction. Hedley enters in a hat and coat and furiously exits the yard as the others watch in silence.

ACT II, Scene 3: Floyd is pacing in the yard when Canewell enters. He is angry and puzzled because Mr. T.L. Hall didn't meet him as planned at the pawn shop with the advance from the Blue Goose. Canewell tells Floyd he should have taken his advice and got more money from his hit record and that now he should demand that Hall and the owner of the Blue Goose cut him in on the profits. Suddenly Red enters bringing bad news for Floyd: Hall has been arrested for selling fake insurance. Floyd bemoans his bad luck in a long speech but concludes, "If I have to buy me a graveyard and kill everybody I see, I am going to Chicago. Floyd Barton is going to Chicago."

ACT II, Scene 4: Red Carter is philosophising about the changes in life and why he is uncomfortable having pawned his pistol. Vera, still making paper flowers, worries about Floyd's long absence. Canewell enters saying only that he has not been able to find Floyd. There is an aura of foreboding heightened by the sudden commotion from a neighbor's yard with a cacaphony of barnyard sounds. Vera says she can only see over the fence that Mrs. Tillery is kneeling down on the ground. Hedley enters in high spirits, singing a different song. He has been to see a black man, Joe

Roberts. Again, he tells that his daddy appeared in a dream, asking forgiveness and promising to send Buddy Bolden with money. Now Hedley is not concerned about the letter from the white man. He dramatically reveals a machete which Roberts has given him to protect himself.

ACT II, Scene 5: Hedley is alone in the yard late at night. Machete in hand, he sings "Ain't no grave . . . can hold my body down" and paces the yard to stay awake. He gives a long, wild tirade, saying the black man isn't a dog in the dust to be kicked, but a lion. He raves of death and destruction. Ruby enters, concerned about the noise he is making. She comes down the stairs and tells him to be quiet, but he continues his raving and tells her that he offers her the chance to be the father of a great man. He is feverish with rage and lust for her and in pity she lifts her dress and gives herself to Hedley as the lights go down.

ACT II, Scene 6: It is now early evening and Floyd is burying something in the garden. He has a new guitar and a dress box. He calls Vera to the window. She asks where he has been for two days and wants to know how he got the money for the guitar and a beautiful dress for her. He says she knows better than to ask, that he had to take a chance so he could get to Chicago and he took it. He shows her the tickets he bought for them to go to Chicago and asks her to marry him. She says she will go with him, but shows him a return ticket, saying, "I hope I never have to use it." He answers, "Well, that's alright."

ACT II, Scene 7: Louise is waiting for the others to go to the Blue Goose. When Vera comes out she starts talking about Ruby and how she went to church with Hedley and talked him into going to the sanitarium to be cured. She says she wouldn't be surprised if there was something between them. When Ruby arrives without Hedley, she says she should have brought him back because he undoubtedly has gone from the church to the moonshine dealer and will be drunk when he returns. Ruby hopes he will live to see her baby born. He is the only man who ever wanted to give her something and she hopes to have a son and call it "King." Canewell enters and is impressed by the appearance of the women. He says a policeman shot Mrs. Tillery's son as he ran from a robbery with another man. They all feel sympathy for Mrs. Tillery, but they turn their thoughts to this evening and Canewell wants to hurry Floyd up. When he is left alone with Vera, she tells him she and Floyd are to be married. He echoes the sense of Floyd's hit song, saying that he loves her, but knows she loves another and wishes her well. Red Carter enters saying the people are arriving and everyone should get down to the Blue Goose. Floyd enters dressed in a fancy white suit he bought in Chicago. Canewell plays his harmonica and announces, "The train is leaving the station." Ruby enters in a sexy red dress and the men stop in their tracks to stare at her.

ACT II, Scene 8: The dance is over and Floyd, Louise, Vera, and Canewell enter talking about how many people there were and what a success they have had. Louise exits and Canewell notices that the Golden Seal plant he gave Vera is out of the ground. Floyd tells Vera to go in the house. As he turns around, Canewell has found the handkerchief full of money he buried. Floyd pulls out his gun and Canewell gives him the money and leaves. Now Floyd stands counting in a shaft of light, illuminating him in his white suit. Hedley enters and is dazzled, laughing and crying, believing that Buddy Bolden has at last come to give him the money. But Floyd refuses to give him the money and shoves him to the ground. Hedley goes to the cellar for his machete and when Floyd stands up after re-burying the money, he kills him, saying, "This time Buddy. . . you give me the money."

ACT II, Scene 9: In the final scene the play returns to the present with the characters sitting in the back yard after the funeral listening to "That's All Right." Vera voices her feelings about the funeral, saying that she saw Floyd rising in the sky and she waved goodbye. She and Louise exit to do the dishes, leaving Canewell and Hedley. Canewell starts the old exchange, "I thought I heard Buddy Bolden say . . ." and Hedley joins in. Canewell asks him what Bolden gave him and Hedley says, "He give me this" showing crumpled money which slips through his fingers like ashes as he continues singing.

Critical Overview--The play opened in New York, 28 March 1996, at the Walter Kerr Theatre (P8.2). Wilson's play was greeted with pleasure by the critics who had been awaiting his next work. In general, the criticism was the same. The play was highly praised, but the first act was seen to be superior to the second and the ending was rather disappointing in contrast to his earlier plays. Responding to the premiere in Chicago (P8.1), King (R169) noted the symbolism connected with Hedley's character and praised Wilson's subtlety and his refusal to sentimentalize the past. Tynan (R172) called the play part bawdy comedy, part dark elegy, and part mystery. Although he enjoyed the characters and the production, he felt the play "slows down and muddies up" in the second half, predicting Wilson would rewrite and improve it. Abarbanel (R167) felt the play exemplified Wilson's unique, richly-styled work, but had too much talk and too much foreshadowing. Kroll (R170) was more positive than most of the other critics, calling Floyd's death shocking but inevitable and saying that the characters are tragic figures "bursting with the balked music of life." When the play opened in New York, Wilson had been rewriting, adding a character and then removing him, and cutting the play throughout 1995 and early 1996. Some critics felt he had not done enough, but Simon (R185), while praising the play on many grounds, felt that Wilson might have "tinkered" with it so much that it had lost its spontaneity. He praised the first act as beautifully written, mordantly witty, and flashing with intensity, but said the second act lacked logic and was frustrating. Nevertheless, he praised the production and was largely positive. Lyons (R184) was more critical, calling the second act sluggish melodrama. Still, he praised much of the play, especially the engaging conversation in the first act. Barnes (R177) said the play lacked clarity and a final punch. However, he praised Wilson and compared him to Chekhov in writing plays of atmosphere, rather than action. Jefferson (R181) was in the camp of those who felt that the second act was weak, but expressed such pleasure about the first act that the impact of the review was positive. Similarly, Kissel (R182) praised the play and said it was full of quiet truth, but was marred by artificial plotting in the second act. Canby (R179) was much more positive, saying the play created a sense that the Broadway season had begun and said that not since *Two Trains Running* and *Angels in America* had the theatre seemed so alive. He called the play a tightly constructed ensemble piece, praised the mood and the acting. He noted some misgivings about the character of Hedley and said the second act seemed slightly out of balance. He concluded that it didn't matter because the rest of the play had such a "grand design." Lahr (R183) was almost entirely positive, writing a rave review--he felt if there were any justice the play would receive the Pulitzer Prize. That prize went to the musical *Rent*, but Wilson received special recognition from the American Theatre Critics Association. He also won the Drama Critics Circle Award for best play. The production and performers were nominated for eight Tony awards. The three-hour play was widely perceived as a success, although not Wilson's best play, and further evidence of his importance in the American theatre.

Two Trains Running (1992)

The Characters--WOLF: a man who has made a success as a numbers runner but who has failed to find one woman to stay with; MEMPHIS: a self-made man, logical and capable, who has worked hard and been honest; RISA: a young, sexy woman who has scarred her legs with a razor, a waitress in Memphis' restaurant who moves very slowly; HOLLOWAY: a man who is outraged at the injustice in the world, but whose belief in the supernatural allows him to pursue life with enjoyment; HAMBONE: forty-two, nearly incapable of speech because of the deterioration of his mind; STERLING: thirty, has just spent five years in prison, wears a prison suit, energetic and straightforward, but sometimes seems unbalanced; WEST: a widower in his sixties, he owns the mortuary across the street and cares only for money.

Plot Summary--ACT I, Scene 1: It is 1969, a morning in Memphis' restaurant in Pittsburgh. Wolf is taking bets on the numbers on the phone and Memphis objects. Memphis has things on his mind including the sale of the building to the government because of urban renewal and the recent departure of his wife because he asked her to make him some bread. Holloway enters with the news that the streets are full of people waiting to see Prophet Samuel in his coffin. They discuss the comparative wealth of the prophet and West, the mortician. Memphis tells how he acquired his building before West could do it and that West has always wanted to buy it. Now Memphis must sell it to the city, but says the city must meet his price. Hambone enters repeating his one phrase, "I want my ham." Risa is concerned about the pathetic man and gives him something to eat and an old coat. Sterling enters, wishing to order some food, but nothing is ready but beans. He takes some coffee and tries to make conversation with Risa, whom he remembers as a skinny girl. He wants to find a job so he won't end up back in the penitentiary but there are no jobs so he is trying to sell his watch. He thinks he will change his luck by standing in line and rubbing Prophet Samuel's head. But Holloway advises him to go see a three hundred and twenty-two year-old woman named Aunt Ester. Memphis jeers at his belief in her age and her ability to change luck, but Sterling sets out to visit her, saying he will return and eat some of Risa's chicken.

ACT I, Scene 2: Wolf is watching the arrival of the white grocer Lutz. Hambone is waiting for him as he does each day to demand his ham. Lutz tells him to take a chicken and goes in the store. Memphis says

Hambone is out of his mind to come each day for nine and a half years demanding payment which he isn't going to get. He says that one day he, himself, will go back down to Natchez to demand the return of his farm, but that he will get it. All he has to do is go down on one of the two trains running every day. When West enters to get his daily coffee and pie, the others ask him about Prophet Samuel and the money which is supposed to be buried with him. West says he will put anything in the casket that anybody wants, but that usually the family gets the jewelry and the money at the last minute. He offers Memphis fifteen thousand dollars for the building, but Memphis says he won't take less than twenty-five thousand. Sterling returns to say that Aunt Ester is sick. He wants Risa to go with him to a rally for Malcolm X. Memphis sneers at the idea of the rally. saying "niggers killed Malcolm . . . and now they want to celebrate his birthday." When Hambone appears, Memphis tells him to take his noise somewhere else and puts him out the door. He says he is tired of hearing Hambone ask for his ham and slams the door.

ACT I, Scene 3: Sterling is eating some of Risa's beans with great appreciation and tells how he was born in an orphanage and has had a hard life. He would like to take Risa to the rally and he would like to dance with her. He says he would protect her at the rally if there is any danger, that in his youth he felt very protective about his sister. He wants to put some money on a number and she tells him seven eighty-one. He says he will play it and if he wins they will get married. Holloway comes in and Sterling says he went over to look at the fence Hambone painted for Lutz and thinks Lutz should have given him the ham for his good work. Wolf enters in high spirits with presents for Risa and Memphis. Sterling tries to borrow money to play the numbers and, failing that, tells Wolf to find him a gun to buy. When Hambone comes in Sterling talks to him and teaches him to say "Black is beautiful." Memphis arrives from the courthouse saying the white people tried to cheat him, but he raised hell and has now got a white lawyer. He talks about the past when he went down to his mother's funeral and returned ready to go somewhere in the world. He says if he has to go out feet first in this struggle, the city will have to meet his price.

ACT II, Scene 1: A flyer for the rally is taped on the wall. Sterling enters bringing Risa some of Prophet Samuel's flowers and carrying a gas can. When Hambone enters, Sterling asks if he remembers the phrases he taught him and they end up shouting "Malcolm lives!" and "I want my ham!" Memphis enters and angrily demands that they stop. Sterling sells him the gas he has "found." Memphis is further irritated by a telephone call from a customer for Wolf. When the latter arrives he has a gun to sell Sterling and Sterling puts his last two dollars on number seven eighty-one. As he exits, Memphis predicts that he will be back in the penitentiary in three weeks. When the phone rings again for Wolf, he angrily tells him it is his place and he doesn't want to be raided for taking numbers. West enters saying the crowd to visit Prophet Samuels has resulted in a broken window. He now offers Memphis twenty thousand for the building. Memphis says he will go down town and get twenty-five thousand, just as he will go down South and get back his farm. Sterling tries to get West to hire him with no success. He has been to see Aunt Ester, but this time she was resting. West explains what happened when he went to see Aunt Ester to find out if his wife had gone to heaven. She told him to take twenty dollars and throw it in the river, but he refused. Holloway says that's why he still doesn't know. In contrast, Holloway threw the money in the river as directed and kept himself from killing his grandfather. Sterling says he is going back to see her and again says that if his number wins he is going to marry Risa. As he exits, Memphis changes his prediction to two weeks.

ACT II, Scene 2: Holloway is worried about Hambone and tells Risa this is the first morning he hasn't been waiting for Lutz in over nine years. Wolf arrives talking about the difficulty with Prophet Samuel's funeral because of the crowds. Wolf is worried because Sterling won but so many people had bet on that number that the white bosses cut the payment in half. Sterling just misses Wolf, having been at the funeral. He says that when he finds Wolf he won't have any more problems. Memphis pays Risa and exits, saying he has to go to the courthouse early and is determined to get his money. At the last moment, he asks Holloway Aunt Ester's address.

ACT II, Scene 3: Risa is sweeping and Holloway is telling about the discovery that Hambone has died and that West has gone to get the body. Risa wants West to bury the body in something better than a welfare casket. Sterling enters still looking for Wolf. He may use the money in a white man's crap game, or take Risa to Vegas, or buy a ranch with horses. But Risa is preoccupied by Hambone's coffin and Sterling is startled to hear he is dead. When Wolf arrives with his bad news, Sterling says now his wedding to Risa will have to be postponed, but that he will go to see the men who run the numbers and demand his money. Risa calls after him, but he is gone.

ACT II, Scene 4: Risa is alone and is very relieved when Sterling appears, again asking her to go to the rally for Malcolm X. He has been to see "the man," and has got satisfaction to the extent of getting back his bet and speaking to Old Man Albertson who was surrounded by bodyguards. He says Albertson gave him the two dollars, but wanted back the $600 Sterling won. Sterling refused and left. Even more importantly, he thinks, he has been to see Aunt Ester who said that Risa has been sent to him by God. He wants to take care of her, but Risa is not interested. When Sterling asks her why she cut her legs, she says she did it because all the men were after her and she wanted to make them ugly. She wants no part of Sterling because she thinks he will rob a bank or end up in the penitentiary. She tells him to go to the rally alone and puts money in the juke box. They start to dance and end up in a passionate embrace, the intensity of which surprises them both.

ACT II, Scene 5: Holloway is talking about love and death and Sterling comes in to report that Hambone looks nice in his coffin, but that only about three or four people have come to see him. They talk about the rally and the fact that the police were there taking photographs. West enters and says that Lutz came by to see Hambone which causes everyone to agree that Lutz is going to rot in hell. Sterling seems to have reached a decision. He gives Wolf the twenty dollars he owes him for the gun and gives Risa what is left of the six hundred dollars he won. After he exits, Wolf asks Risa what is going on between them, but she pays him no mind. Memphis enters drunk and ready to celebrate for he has gone to Aunt Ester's, taken her advice, thrown the money in the river, and subsequently got thirty-five thousand dollars from the city for his building. When he finds out that Hambone has died, he expresses sorrow that Lutz never gave him his ham and orders fifty dollars worth of flowers as a tribute from all of them. He recovers his high spirits and talks about following Aunt Ester's advice and going back to get his farm. Then he will return and open up a fancy restaurant. Suddenly there is the sound of breaking glass and a burglar alarm. Then a bloody, but triumphant, Sterling enters with a ham stolen from Lutz and gives it to West for Hambone's casket.

Critical Overview--*Two Trains Running* opened following the staged reading, the New Haven run and presentations in several cities on 13 April 1992 at the Walter Kerr Theatre (P9.2). Critics had a mixed reaction to *Two Trains Running* with several complaining that it had a rambling quality. Most critics noted that Wilson did not foreground the political activities of the '60s, but many felt that was a good choice. Almost all critics gave high praise to the actors, particularly Larry Fishburne and Roscoe Lee Browne. There were several critics who praised all aspects of the evening, reaffirming Wilson's high position in the American theatre. Beaufort (R125) said the play was the kind of success which would add to Wilson's already prestigious laurels. He advised the audience to enjoy the fragments of dialogues and incidents which the talented author knew how to blend into a meaningful collage. He noted that the play unfolds smoothly in two acts and is the most comic of Wilson's plays. More than just a play, Wilson's work is an experience. Simon (R130) regarded the play as a positive step forward for Wilson, whose earlier plays involved onstage violence, ponderous symbols, and supernatural phenomena. Like many other critics, he found the symbolism of the two trains, life and death, meaningful and carefully worked out. Ultimately, he praised the writing, staging, and acting. Surprisingly, Stearns (R131) called the acting great and praised the three-hour long play as well-focused and combining comedy and tragedy with breathtaking elegance. Ansen (R123) voiced similar feelings, and praised the play as a presentation of the stories behind the obvious political slogans of the 1960s, dramatically discursive, but musically eloquent and a challenge to the audience. In a short review in *Time*, Henry (R126) gave solid praise to all aspects, calling the play Wilson's most delicate and mature work revealing clearly that Wilson is a poet. In a very long analysis of the positive impact of the play, Richards (R129) called it Wilson's funniest and most benevolent play to date, filled with interesting characters beautifully performed. He felt there was an amorphous quality but that the "flavorsome talk" made it acceptable and the fact that nothing in particular happened in the play was a meaningful comment about the 1960s in retrospect. But his colleague on the *New York Times*, Rich (R128), while praising the language and Wilson's experimental "will to demolish the well-made play," complained about repetition and heavy metaphorical use as well as a failure to delve deeply enough into the characters of Risa and Sterling. Still, he concluded that the play was fascinating. Barnes (R124) was more negative, heading the review "'Trains' Doesn't Run." Despite the excellent acting and attractive elements in the play, the work was not in focus, and had less immediacy and more padding than the earlier plays. Ultimately, it did not offer edification for white audiences. Kissel (R127) agreed that the play lacked action and said it did not make enough comment on the 1960s. Nevertheless, he said the play was always interesting because of Wilson's gift for language and the fine performances. Critic Wilson (R133) was essentially in agreement with this view, while praising the poetry and playwright Wilson's unfailing talent for dialogue and storytelling, he faulted the absence of a unifying struggle which would move the plot forward. Nevertheless, he described Wilson as the outstanding American playwright of the past decade. Watt (R132), too, called it a plotless play whose parts never cohered despite the performances, but said, also, that it was never dull. Saying the same thing, but in a positive response was Winer (R134) who wrote a long analysis praising the play. Admitting that some theatre-goers might find the play too long and talky, she defended it and Wilson's whole cycle, saying that in his five plays he has populated the stage with memorable characters who refuse to be forgotten. At this point in Wilson's career, then, Wilson was considered a major American playwright, there was continued respect for his talent and his aims, delight in his language and characterization, but concern about the length and structure of the play. Fishburne won a Tony award and Wilson received a nomination for the Tony award for the best play. He did not win that but was awarded the American Theatre Critics' Association Award for Best Play and the Drama Critics Circle Award for Best Play. These awards indicate the high regard in which critics throughout America hold Wilson's work. Following the New York production the play toured to Chicago where it was warmly received.

Primary Bibliography

This section is divided into two subsections, locating Wilson's original writings: Non-Dramatic Works and Dramatic Publications.

NON-DRAMATIC PRIMARY WORKS

The following is an alphabetically ordered primary bibliography of Wilson's non-fiction, published material, designated by the prefix "A."

A 01   "August Wilson Responds." *American Theatre* October 1996: 101-107.
        Wilson makes a lengthy response to Brustein's "Subsidized Separatism." Says the critic denies universality to artists who explore their lives as African Americans. "His bias blinds him to the fact that being a black artist isn't 'limiting' any more than being a white artist is." Says Brustein is irresponsible in his language, "makes false and spurious accusations," and denies factual information. Corrects some misquotations. Clarifies Wilson's views about other black playwrights and about critics, and denies he ever said he wouldn't allow a white director to do his plays.

A02   "Characters Behind History Teach Wilson About Plays." *New York Times* 12 Apr. 1992, sec. 2: 5.
        Discusses his rising interest in history in 7th grade. It is not surprising that he intends to write a play for each decade of the 20th century. Idea came to him after he wrote two plays and it empowered him. He is restoring the experience of blacks

to a primary position. As an artist wants to "fashion of the
finest gold the proper angel."

A03   "The Ground on Which I Stand." *American Theatre* Sept.
           1996: 14-16, 71-74.
                   The text of the address Wilson presented as keynote
           speaker at the Theatre Communications Group National
           Conference. An eloquent statement of his beliefs--he says he
           speaks only for himself--about black theatre and its needs.
           Discusses his involvement with the Black Power movement
           "the kiln in which I was fired." Says of the 66 LORT theatres
           only one, the Crossroads Theater, is black. Says black theatre
           is alive, vibrant, and vital--it just isn't funded. Funds to white
           theatres to do black plays is a form of cultural imperialism
           which diverts money from black theatres. Attacks Brustein for
           "sophomoric assumptions" about minority theatre, establishing
           a presumption of inferiority in these works. Says we do not
           need colorblind casting, need theatres to develop black
           playwrights. Calls for a meeting of black playwrights in 1998
           in the South to prepare to enter the "millenium united and
           prepared' for future prosperity. Says Brustein is wrong to make
           charges of separatism and calls for an "unencumbered pursuit
           of happiness to the ground on which we all stand."

A04   "Great Goals." *Time* 15 Oct. 1992: 74.
                   Wilson's position as a known playwright is now such
           that he has been asked as one of 16 internationally known
           figures to say what mankind should accomplish in coming
           decades. Wilson says we should make greed the worst sin and
           shun greedy people all over the planet. Greed is the basis of all
           society's problems.

A05   "How to Write a Play Like August Wilson." *New York Times*
           10 Mar. 1991, Sec. 2: 5.
                   Tells how he got his first typewriter and how he writes
           on napkins in bars and restaurants. Starts a play with a line of
           dialogue, then asks his characters questions. Sometimes he is
           surprised by the turns the plot takes because of discoveries he
           makes about the characters. He listens to them talking to him

and gradually puts together a total picture. Characters are all invented but made up out of himself, although his plays are not autobiographical. Discussion of the themes in his plays. Discusses ending of *The Piano Lesson* and the controversy about it. He defends the choices he made related to the ending and the characters. His favorite of those he has written is *Joe Turner's Come and Gone*.

A06   "I Want a Black Director." *New York Times* 26 Sept. 1990: 25A.

In 1987 Paramount bought rights to film *Fences* with Eddie Murphy, but Wilson wants a black director. He can't understand why people reject his idea. Presents a lengthy justification for insisting on a black director and explains why he rejected a well-known white director on cultural grounds: he feels the white director would be an outsider in relationship to black culture and to the screenplay. He also discusses other ethnic groups and suggests that blacks should not direct Italian films, Italians not direct Jewish films, etc. He believes executives at Paramount distrust the abilities of blacks and are therefore reluctant to hire a black director.

A07   "In His Own Words." *Applause--Denver Center for the Performing Arts* Jan. 1990: 5.

Discusses the importance of black history and need to educate children about it. Discusses racism as a theme in *Fences*. Says he wanted to show that whites are wrong to characterize black men as "lazy and shiftless" and to show a man who "has responsibilities as prime to his life." Charming anecdote about his view of prizes he has won--he says, "August, they're all important, no matter where they come from."

A08   "The Legacy of Malcolm X." *Life* Dec. 1992: 84.

Discussion of Malcolm's death and the changes for the worse in his neighborhood since that time. Says this street was the center of a bustling neighborhood when he delivered papers there as a boy. Now he cannot safely walk there. Feels Malcolm had much to say that was logical and valuable. Talks about developing Afrocentric reality, reemergence of Malcolm as a cultural icon. There is a shift from the attention to the teachings of Martin Luther King, Jr., to those of Malcolm. Blacks need to have the power to control essential and simple aspects of their lives.

A09   "Notes to *Ma Rainey's Black Bottom*." New York: Manhattan Records, SVB0 53001: 1985.
          Introduction to original Broadway cast recording. Wilson describes his life in a rooming house in Pittsburgh where he first heard Ma Rainey sing "Nobody in Town Can Bake a Sweet Jellyroll Like Mine" and discovered his "full presence in the world." In this rooming house, which in a way he never really left, he was influenced by phonograph records of the blues which he bought at a St. Vincent de Paul store for five cents each. Discussion of coming to manhood and his beliefs. Discusses the ideas he wanted to express in this play. Excellent photos from the New York production.

DRAMATIC PUBLICATIONS

The following is a list of texts in which Wilson's plays have been individually published, collected, or anthologized. Although Wilson wrote some plays before *Ma Rainey's Black Bottom*, he has said he doesn't intend to continue work on most of them and they have not been published.

FENCES

          Fences. New York: New American Library, 1986.
          Fences and Ma Rainey's Black Bottom. Harmondsworth, England: Penguin, 1988.
          Three Plays. Pittsburgh: University of Pittsburgh Press, 1991.

Anthologies:
          Best Plays of 1986-87. Eds. Otis L. Guernsey and Jeffrey Sweet. New York: Dodd, 1988.

Black Theatre USA. Eds. James B. Hatch and Ted Shine. New York: Free Press, 1996.

The Compact Bedford Introduction to Drama. Ed. Lee A. Jacobus. Boston: Bedford Books, 1996.

JOE TURNER'S COME AND GONE

Joe Turner's Come and Gone. New York: New American Library, 1988.

Three Plays. Pittsburgh: University of Pittsburgh Press, 1991.

Anthology:

Best Plays of 1987-88. Eds. Otis L. Guernsey and Jeffrey Sweet. New York: Dodd, 1989.

MA RAINEY'S BLACK BOTTOM

Ma Rainey's Black Bottom. New York: New American Library, 1985.

Fences and Ma Rainey's Black Bottom. Harmondsworth, England: Penguin, 1988.

Three Plays. Pittsburgh: University of Pittsburgh Press, 1991.

Anthologies:

Best Plays of 1984-85, ed. Otis L. Guernsey and Jeffrey Sweet. New York: Dodd, 1986.

Totem Voices: Plays from the Black World Repertory. New York: Grove Press, 1989.

THE PIANO LESSON

The Piano Lesson. New York: Plume, 1990.

Anthology:

Best Plays of 1989-90. Eds. Otis L. Guernsey and Jeffrey Sweet. New York: Dodd, 1991.

SEVEN GUITARS

   Seven Guitars. New York: Samuel French, 1996.

Anthology:
   Best Plays of 1995-96. Eds. Otis L. Guernsey and Jeffrey Sweet.
      New York: Dodd, 1993.

TWO TRAINS RUNNING

   Two Trains Running. New York: Dutton, 1992.
   Two Trains Running. New York: Plume, 1993.
   Two Trains Running. New Jersey: Penguin, 1996.

Anthology:
   Best Plays of 1991-92. Eds. Otis L. Guernsey and Jeffrey Sweet.
      New York: Dodd, 1993.

Secondary Bibliography

The following is an exhaustive, annotated secondary bibliography concentrating on Wilson's career in the theatre. Biographical material is also of central concern and included.

The bibliography is chronologically ordered. Within each included year, entries are divided into three categories: (1) "Reviews": articles that specifically refer to a then currently running performance, designated "R"; (2) "Articles, Chapters, Sections": separate texts that discuss Wilson and/or his work, or sections of larger texts not exclusively dedicated to Wilson and his craft, designated "S"; and (3) "Book-Length Studies": works dedicated to Wilson and his craft, also designated "S."

Every effort has been made to provide full bibliographical information and to suggest alternate sources for hard-to-find texts, when available. In some instances, particularly in the case of older newspaper reviews, page numbers were unavailable and, unfortunately, occasionally are omitted.

1984-1989

1984

Reviews

R001   Barnes, Clive. "'Ma Rainey'--The Black Experience." *New York Post* 12 Oct. 1984. In *New York Theatre Critics' Reviews*, 1984. 197.

Says it is a slice of life and a rather strange play in terms of construction. It is very much a political play. Ma Rainey inspired Wilson, but she is not the center of the play. The musicians' struggle against the white bosses is. Praises Richards' direction. But says the play has a crucial fault in that nothing much happens. The play is never really there, but the fine acting makes the audience forget that.

R002   Beaufort, John. "Plight of 1920s Blacks Superbly Portrayed in New Wilson Drama." *Christian Science Monitor* 16 Oct. 1984. In *New York Theatre Critics' Reviews*, 1984. 198.
            Ma Rainey is a bravura figure in the drama, but the focus is on the band. Its activity becomes a metaphor for Wilson's examination of "black musicians' plight" in a period of intense racism. Play is filled with deep insights and spontaneous humor. Superb acting and staging. Critic notes excellence of the Yale Repertory Theatre production now playing on Broadway.

R003   Hawley, David. "Penumbra's 'Jitney' Is Early but Worthwhile Play by Wilson." *St. Paul Pioneer Press* Dec. 1984.
            Describes it as a one-act unsophisticated sketch whose weaknesses are apparent, but direction by Claude Purdy fine, acting good, characters interesting and some powerful moments. One is seldom bored in the 80-minute performance.

R004   Kissel, Howard. Rev. of *Ma Rainey's Black Bottom. Women's Wear Daily* 12 Oct. 1984. In *New York Theatre Critic' Reviews*, 1984. 200.
            The play and the performance by Dutton are both comic and unsettling. Cast is excellent and Dutton gives a shattering performance. Dialogue is fresh and avoids familiar jargon. It has wit and a clear musical shape. This is a play of great power, presented with grace and sensitivity.

R005   Kroll, Jack. "So Black and Blue." *Newsweek* 12 Oct. 1984. In *New York Theatre Critics' Reviews*, 1984: 199-200.

         Initial expectations are humorous, but Wilson subverts them with dramatic irony and the play becomes "a microcosm of the subjugation of black Americans." It is fierce and biting, but not grim because it is filled with humor. Wilson reveals the tormented spirit of Ma Rainey. Levee's actions trigger a shocking climax. Actors are generally marvelous, but Dutton is astonishing as Levee. Merritt perfect as Ma Rainey. Director Richards has great sensitivity.

R006   "'Ma Rainey's Black Bottom' Is A Winner On Broadway." *Jet* 12 Nov. 1984: 62, 64.

         Talks about the themes in the play noting that it is about black-white relationships and about black self-hatred caused by racism. Merritt commendable as Ma, but most of the tension and action centers around the musicians played with gusto and grace, with Dutton especially moving. The play works, the language is rich, the motions true, and the direction on target. Rare to see a black drama on Broadway, so critic hopes it will have a long run.

R007   Rich, Frank. Rev. of *Ma Rainey's Black Bottom*. *New York Times* 11 Apr. 1984: 1C.

         Wilson is a major find for American theatre. Events in play are invented, but rooted in fact. Play, at Yale Rep, is a paradigmatic drama of black aspirations with an explosive ending. Excellent production excepting nephew and white characters. Dutton and Merritt superb.

R008   Rich, Frank. "Wilson's 'Ma Rainey's' Open." *New York Times* 12 Oct. 1984. In *New York Theatre Critics' Reviews*, 1984. 196-197.

         A very long review which says Wilson sends the entire history of black America crashing down on our heads. Harrowing, but also funny. Richards was "born to direct it." Speeches are like improvised musical solos.

Gives a long description of Dutton's "red-hot" performance as Levee. All the actors play instruments and act miraculously well. Wilson has created art out of suffering.

R009   Siegel, Joel. Review of *Ma Rainey*. WABC-TV 11 Oct. 1984. In *New York Theatre Critics' Reviews*, 1984. 196-197.

Dialogue is musical and in perfect pitch. Wilson is both funny and serious, but shifts too suddenly to serious points. Play has flaws, but as theatre is "fireworks." Dutton, just out of school, gives one of finest Broadway debuts critic has ever seen.

R010   Simon, John. "Black Bottom, Black Sheep." *New York Post* 22 Oct. 1984: 95.

While he has little to say that is positive about this play, he does note that Wilson is a new black playwright with promise. Generally negative review notes both flaws in play and production. Says that the play, as a play, is only "intermittently drama" and that Wilson should have developed the structure and characters more fully.

R011   Taylor, Markland. "'Ma Rainey' Uneven but Disarming." *New Haven Register* 8 Apr. 1984: 1.

Essentially positive review but two major objections. Too much fun and too many speeches by musicians in early part of the play blunts impact of ending. It needs cutting. Imbalance results with too little focus on Ma. Actress should have had more opportunity. Exciting production features excellent acting in all roles.

R012   Watt, Douglas. "'Ma Rainey's': Mostly It Swings." *Daily News* 12 Oct. 1984. In *New York Theatre Critics' Reviews*, 1984. 197.

Calls it a superb production in all ways. Tendency toward wordiness compensated for by acting. Entertaining most of the time, but really more of a slice of life than a play. It is really about the four musicians, not Ma Rainey. All four are unforgettable, but Dutton stands out moving from fun to a horrifying scene. He is magnificant and the others not far behind. Critic has some reservations about factuality of play and found some dull moments.

R013   Wilson, Edwin. "On Broadway: 'Ma Rainey.'" *Wall Street Journal* 16 Oct. 1984. In *New York Times Theatre Critics' Reviews*, 1984. 199.

There is a pleasing atmosphere and interesting banter, but not much of a play. Musicians are waiting and so is the audience. Theme of play is racial injustice, but "polemics don't make a play." There isn't even enough music--only two songs. The evening is interesting, though, because the first-rate cast and direction make up for shortcomings.

Articles, Chapters, Sections

S014   Hawley, David. "Spotlight on Penumbra; August Wilson Escorts 'Jitney!' to St. Paul." *St. Paul Pioneer Press* 9 Dec. 1984: 3E, 36E.

The Jerome Foundation announced an annual new playwriting contest. The first winner is *Jitney*. Company arranged to present the early Wilson play before he became "one of America's hottest new playwrights." Now Wilson is writing *The Piano Lesson* with the help of a McKnight Fellowship. Wilson discusses origins of *Jitney* in actual experiences in Pittsburgh.

S015   Jackson, Caroline. "August Wilson: Survivor/Poet/ Playwright." *Black Masks* Nov. 1984: 1, 8-9.

Biographical sketch describing the several stages of his career: his family background, his youth in Pittsburgh, his problems in high school. A sympathetic portrait of an important figure in contemporary black culture whose plays are attracting attention. First of a series of articles in this journal about his life and work.

S016   Mitgang, Herbert. "Wilson, From Poetry to Broadway Success; 'Ma Rainey's' Is First Hit for Author." *New York Times* 22 Oct. 1984: 15C.

                 Writer speaks with Wilson and with Richards who describes him as "already a major playwright, not for black theatre, but for American theatre." Survey of 39-year-old playwright's life and career. Interesting quotes from Wilson about his past, many specific details of his life. Describes genesis of *Ma Rainey* and its development. Predicts a major career in theatre.

S017   Powers, Kim. "An Interview With August Wilson." *Theater* Fall/Winter 1984: 50-55.

                 Interview follows Wilson's success at Yale and on Broadway. Wilson describes importance of poetry in his writing, his concern with black history, his positive attitude about the black playwrights of the 70s, then answers many questions about forthcoming *Joe Turner*. The new play is based on a real historical figure who mistreated black persons in the South.

1985

Reviews

R018   Gold, Sylviane. "August Wilson Escapes the Sophomore Jinx." *Wall Street Journal* 10 May 1985.

                 Says second plays and novels often fail, but *Fences* succeeds and is better crafted and more satisfying dramatically, although more conventional. Presents a psychological portrait of urban blacks in late '50s. Character of Troy and interpretation by Jones rich, but wife and brother derivative characters. Moving story line and a central character almost Shakespearean in contour.

R019   Johnson, Malcolm L. "'Fences' Is Riveting at Yale Rep." *Hartford Courant* 5 May 1985.

Play is a success, presents failed dreams and conflicting values. Jones dominates play as a "Lear whose domain is small" moving from jollity to rage, but whole cast fine. Play combines humor and anger. Play is always riveting, but is rambling and discursive. Language slangy and poetic.

R020   Massa, Robert. "Fence Mechanisms." *Village Voice* May 1985.
Feels play has been overpraised by some critics, Wilson is weak at dramatic structure. His work fails in many ways so it is wrong to praise his work so highly. As a white viewer, the critic objects to some aspects of Wilson's approach. Ending is derivative and resembles *Death of a Salesman.* Mary Alice and James Earl Jones are excellent. Play could have been cut to a one-act and been a stronger work.

Articles, Chapters, Sections

S021   Freedman, Samuel G. "Wilson's New 'Fences' Nurtures a Partnership." *New York Times* 5 May 1985.
First play announced arrival of stirring new writer. Discusses difficulties of writing second play after such success. Description of warm relationship with Richards and how he and Wilson work together, particularly in the area of cutting. Richards is a nurturing factor in Wilson's career.

S022   Henderson, Heather. "Building *Fences*: An Interview with Mary Alice and James Earl Jones." *Theater* Summer/Fall 1985: 67-70.
Follows performance of play. Writer asks the actors to discuss working with Richards and developing the play. They find the dialogue to be true. Wilson loves actors so even small roles are interesting. They know these characters as people. As an actor, Jones misses acting a resolution scene with Troy because he does not appear in the last act.

S023   Killen, Tom. "A Black Family's Struggle in Wilson Work at Rep." *New Haven Register* 28 Apr. 1985.

   Says Wilson came out of nowhere and took Broadway by storm with first play, but was not concerned about critical response to next play, just exhilarated and eager to write more. "Fences" reflects his concern that his generation did not understand the suffering of his parents generation. Wilson's own experience growing up is expressed. He says the parents hid the daily indignities inflicted upon them. Talks about his early life and writing.

1986

Reviews

R024   Johnson, Malcolm L. "Yale Rep's 'Joe Turner' Develops Slowly." *Hartford Courant* May 1986.

   Says strains in play seem not to come together in first act, but Wilson pulls them tight in the next. A complex and poetic play which grips the audience. Dutton is excellent as Loomis. Director Richards fails to build tension and mystery in first act. Ed Hall, last minute replacement as Bynum, wrong for role.

R025   Rich, Frank. "'Joe Turner' at Yale Rep." *New York Times* 6 May 1986.

   Dutton a Dickensian figure of doom and mystery as Loomis. Play is potentially Wilson's finest. A search for identity which is rich in religious feeling and historical detail. Excellent development of relationship between Bynum and Loomis. Sad story is filled with humor and hypnotic story-telling as grittily redolent as those in *The Iceman Cometh*. Still needs fine tuning in relation to final scene.

R026   Taylor, Markland. "Premiere Seems a Bit Premature." *New Haven Register* 4 May 1986.

Says play is an improvement over "Fences" which was too openly derivative of Arthur Miller and *Joe Turner* is far more original. But the play is unorganized and roles of children could be cut. Total structure needs to be tightened. Wilson has failed to do enough work since staged reading at O'Neill Center in 1984.

Articles, Chapters, Sections

S027   Altman, Peter. "An Interview with August Wilson." *Huntington Theatre Company Spotlight* September-October 1986: 1-3.
            Joe Turner at the Huntington Theatre in Boston. Wilson answers questions about his life and friendship with Claude Purdy who encouraged him to write plays and move to Minneapolis. Talks about working as a cook while writing plays. Discussion of genesis of *Joe Turner*. Wilson says he loves the play and hopes that by pointing out the difference in white and black sensibilities, he will cause whites to see blacks differently.

S028   Kleiman, Dena. "'Joe Turner,' The Spirit of Synergy." *New York Times* 10 May 1986: 11C.
            Writer interviews Wilson in New Haven where new play, *Joe Turner's Come and Gone*, has opened to some rave reviews and has pleased audiences. Discusses rewriting process, cutting and developing, with suggestions from director Richards. Wilson says the play is about healing and about identity. It is an important play for blacks, but has a universal message.

S029   Moore Jr. , David. "Joe Turner's Come and Gone." *Yale Repertory Theatre Newsletter* Vol. X, no. 6, 1986: 1-3.
            Discusses real Joe Turner and Wilson's response to the person. Wilson's plays tell us about the pasts of individuals and collectively about the past of a race. Wilson's examination of the relationship of blacks to their myths important in the plays. New play another important collaboration of Wilson and Richards.

S030   Smith II, Philip E. *"Ma Rainey's Black Bottom*: Playing
            the Blues as Equipment for Living." *Within the Dramatic
            Spectrum*. Ed. Karelisa V. Hartigan. New York: University
            Press of America: 1986.
                Wilson's play is a playing of the blues "wherein
            language, representation, and action on stage encompass
            several kinds of blues performances." Gives a history of
            the blues and the way in which they help the characters in
            the play to live. Close analysis of the characters and the
            action of the play. It is ultimately about the relationship of
            self to history and culture.

                                    1987

                                   Reviews

R031   Barnes, Clive. "Fiery 'Fences.'" *New York Post* 27 Mar.
            1987. In *New York Times Theatre Critics' Reviews*, 1987:
            316.
                Strong emotional response to play, he was not
            merely moved, but transfixed. Wrong to call Wilson a
            "'black' playwright because the plays are classic American
            drama with strong tragic elements. "It is the strongest,
            most passionate American dramatic writing since
            Tennessee Williams." Troy Maxson will be remembered as
            one of the great characters of American theatre and James
            Earl Jones as the first actor to play him.

R032   Beaufort, John. "'Fences' Probes Life of Blacks in '50s."
            Christian Science Monitor 27 Mar. 1987. In *New York
            Theatre Critics' Reviews*, 1987. 318.
                A play of depth, eloquence, and power which adds
            stature to current season. The center is the magnificent
            performance by James Earl Jones. Mary Alice is excellent
            and to see them together is a "profound experience." The
            production is splendid and entire cast excellent. Play
            blends the unique and the universal.

R033   Disch, Thomas M. Rev. of *Fences*. *Nation* 18 Apr. 1987: 516-517.

Says too much hype about play: press has treated play as "a kind of coronation ceremony" for Wilson. He liked it less than *Ma Rainey*. It is a one-man show with Troy "gassing" like some garrulous drunk. Says both the play and the author are overrated. The implication is that critics praise Wilson because he is black.

R034   Hawley, David. "Local 'Ma Rainey' Takes a Different Tack." *St. Paul Pioneer Press* 9 May 1987: 5B.

Play is one of best productions in Penumbra Theatre history. Notes Wilson's long connection with the theatre. Production is smaller in scale than Broadway production but also different in interpretation. The passionate play is even hotter and yet more humorous. Notes Wilson's long connection with the theatre. Local premiere of this play.

R035   Henry III, William A. "Righteous in His Own Backyard." *Time* 6 Apr. 1987. In *New York Theatre Critics' Reviews*, 1987. 320-21.

Notes critical and popular success of *Ma Rainey* and gives information about Wilson's life. Fences is a picture of a garbage man which is vividly particular, but which reflects the tragedy of a generation. Great performance by James Earl Jones. Play is a major step forward for Wilson, the most impassioned and authentic new voice since Mamet.

R036   Jones, Sumner. Rev. *Ma Rainey's Black Bottom*. Unident. Minneapolis newspaper, May 1987.

Play is a masterful depiction by a very talented artist. Production typical of good work at the Penumbra Theatre, light touch by director Claude Purdy. Exciting, provocative theatre with a company capable of performing it well. Theatre has produced several Wilson plays. Raucous humor blends well with the serious material and whole production is very satisfying.

R037   Kissel, Howard. "One Man's Failure Is Another Man's
            Smash." *Daily News* 27 Mar. 1987. In *New York Theatre
            Critics' Reviews*, 1987. 315.
                     Fences is powerful and it is one of James Earl
            Jones' most impressive performances. Dialogue has a
            deeply musical quality; Wilson one of the few American
            playwrights one can call a poet. The performances are
            joyous and the language enobles the characters' troubling
            lives. Although the play is long, it is a blockbuster--a
            "major American play passionately performed."

R038   Kroll, Jack. "Nine Innings Against the Devil." *Newsweek* 6
            Apr. 1987. In *New York Theatre Critics' Reviews*, 1987.
            34.
                     James Earl Jones demonstrates what great acting
            is and uses all his range as Troy. *Fences* is not as exciting
            as *Ma Rainey* as it lacks its "raw cutting edge." Richards
            brings out fine performances and has complete
            understanding of the play. Wilson is a leading new voice
            in American theatre, but he should work for new forms "to
            deal with the new twists and turns of a troubled black
            destiny."

R039   Lida, David. Rev. of *Fences. Women's Wear Daily* 27
            Mar. 1987. In *New York Theatre Critics' Reviews*, 1987.
            321.
                     Wilson has one of the finest ears for language in
            the theatre and writes with rolling, fluid rhythms. Play is
            filled with funny lines and powerful phrases. But critic
            wanted less talk and more action. Finds a major fault
            structurally to have discussion of Alberta (who bears Troy
            a child) who never appears. Play is rewarding for the
            language and the acting.

R040   Rich, Frank. "Family Ties in Wilson's 'Fences.'" *New
            York Times* 27 Mar. 1987. In *New York Theatre Critics'
            Reviews*, 1987. 314.

May be James Earl Jones' best role to date. Character runs the range of rage, delicacy, and gravity. Powerful play with fine acting throughout. Discusses central conflict between Troy and son which is very American. Play is tame compared to the "firecracker" *Ma Rainey* but has gripping second act. Play leaves no doubt that Wilson is a major writer with humor and a passionate commitment to the great subject of history. Universal theme appeals to theatregoers.

R041   Siegel, Joel. Rev. of *Fences*. WABC-TV 26 Mar. 1987. In *New York Theatre Critics' Reviews*, 1987. 321.

Characterization of Troy is what is rarely seen on stage: a whole man who is alive. *Ma Rainey* was excellent and now Wilson has written a great play. Cast and set excellent. Some delays between scenes, but otherwise direction perfect. Play is rare meeting of part and player "that makes theatre history."

R042   Taylor, Markland. "Yale Rep's 'The Piano Lesson' Needs Considerable Fine Tuning." *New Haven Register* Dec. 1987.

Play is in rougher shape than earlier two plays when premiered. Needs clarifying and cutting, must find dramatic center. Both director and playwright need to improve production. Ending noisy and unsatisfactory. Samuel I. Jackson tiresome as Boy Willie and Carl Gordon unsure as Doaker. Good scene when characters sing a work song, but on the whole the play is not a success particularly in the acting of the central role.

R043   Wallach, Allan. "Fenced in by a Lifetime of Resentments." *New York Newsday* 27 Mar. 1987. In *New York Theatre Critics' Reviews*, 1987. 319.

Discusses character of Troy and rich portrayal by James Earl Jones. Playwright made a remarkable playwriting debut with *Ma Rainey*, but this is not as good. There is less excitement. Play is more conventional. But Wilson's ear for rhythms of the characters is displayed.

Praise for setting and Richards' directing despite some "languid moments." A rather ambiguous review.

R044   Watt, Douglas. "'Fences' Is All Over the Lot." *Daily News* 3 Apr. 1987. In *New York Theatre Critics' Reviews*, 1987. 316.

James Earl Jones' performance is so magnificent that the play must be seen. Wilson shows gift for powerful individual scenes, but less for a cohesive play. Structure and characterization needed work. Evening is a genre piece with interesting characters and fine performances and that is not enough. Unfortunately Wilson has written only a "genre piece delineating character."

R045   Weales, Gerald. "Bringing the Light." *Commonweal* 22 May 1987: 320-21.

Thoughtful analysis of *Fences*. Says Wilson stretches the limit of the realistic form in *Fences*. There is verisimilitude in his plays, but also a lyric quality. The play has a strong use of metaphor. Discusses the character of Troy who has "strength, a sense of duty, and an odd vulnerability." He fills the play even in the last act which follows his death.

R046   Wilson, David. "An Unfinished Symphony." *New Haven Advocate* 7 Dec. 1987.

The Piano Lesson is haunting and haunted with shades of memory and phantoms of fear and ghosts. Play is rich and provocative, elevating drama to literature and scope, language, and rhythms are wholly majestic. Problems exist which Wilson must address: too long, ending unsatisfactory. Wilson and Richards should work to improve it before taking it to Broadway. Superior cast with fine direction by Richards at Yale Rep.

R047   Wilson, Edwin. "Wilson's 'Fences' on Broadway . . . " *Wall Street Journal* 31 Mar. 1987. In *New York Theatre Critics' Reviews*, 1987. 317.

Play contains scenes which only a real dramatist could conceive. Strikes at the heart not only of the black experience, but human condition. Discusses symbolism of the fence. Symbolically it relates to fences in the lives of the characters who often want to escape them. Not a polemical piece, rather a universal quality. Play is particularly welcome addition to season.

Articles, Chapters, Sections

S048   Arkatov, Janice. "August Wilson: His Way." *Los Angeles Times* 7 June 1987: 35-36.

Notes that *Fences* is nominated for six Tony Awards. Quotes Wilson about his life and career. "I'm an artist first, a playwright second, and a black third." Also, "I'm writing about the stuff that beats in my head." Wilson emphasizes that poetry is the foundation on which he approaches his plays.

S049   DeVries, Hilary. "A Song In Search of Itself." *American Theatre* Jan. 1987: 22-25.

Long analysis of Wilson's life, outlooks, and plays. Says Wilson is a chronicler of black America's recent past. Playwright defends his intention to write about black characters. Wilson has emerged as a playwright who will still be influential in the decades to come. Good descussion of Wilson's plays and good photos of productions.

S050   Freedman, Samuel G. "A Voice From the Streets." *New York Times Magazine* 15 Mar. 1987: 36, 40, 49, 50.

Says Wilson's ambition is to be recognized by people in the slum in Pittsburgh as their voice. Good picture of Wilson's early life with many details. Notes influence of painter Romare Bearden. Says Wilson feels black playwrights are advised to "Leave your Africanness outside." Discusses his plan for a cycle of plays set in each decade of the century.

S051   Gerard, Jeremy. "'Misérables' and 'Fences' Win Top
        Awards." *New York Times* 8 June 1987: 1.
              Fences won four Tonys out of six nominations:
        best play, best direction, best actor, and featured actress
        beating strong competition. Short piece of information.

S052   Harris, Alison. "Links to the Past." Program for *Joe
        Turner* at Seattle Repertory Theatre Jan. 1987: 9-10.
              Herald Loomis takes his characters back to
        voodoo and beyond. Talks about slaves brought to
        America and the background of the play and the role of
        conjurers in slave life. The vision Loomis has in the play
        reveals to him that he is the descendent of the slaves--he
        has heard a voice from another continent.

S053   "'Fences' by St. Paul Playwright Wins 4 Tonys, Including
        Best Play." *Minneapolis Star Tribune* 8 June 1987: 10A.
              Associated Press release covering Tony Awards.
        Notes Wilson's intention to write cycle of plays set in each
        decade of twentieth century. Gives summary of Wilson's
        career and notes that two other actors in the Wilson play
        were nominated for awards.

S054   Jackson, Caroline. "'Fences: The Odyssey of a Play."
        Black Masks Feb./Mar. 1987: 4, 11.
              Author questions Wilson about the genesis and
        production history of *Fences*. Considers the portrait of
        Troy Maxson and his position in society. Close
        description of work done on the play in its progress from
        the O'Neill Center staged reading, through regional
        productions, and Broadway opening. Considers the play
        an important milestone in black theatre.

S055   Jackson, Caroline. "James Earl Jones: Triumphant Again."
        Black Masks Feb./Mar. 1987: 2-3, 11.
              Follow-up on *Fences* with questions for Jones
        about his interpretation of the role, his feelings about
        performing it, and his views of the significance of the
        play. Jones discusses his view of the character and the

difficulties he encountered, particularly with the absence of a final scene. Jones presents a picture of his whole career on stage. Good view of Wilson's work from the point of view of an actor.

S056   Killen, Tom. "Black Theater Triumphant." *The World and I* Dec. 1987: 236-239.
        Wilson is one of the most important playwrights to appear in years. Discusses success of Wilson's plays. His symbiotic relationship with Richards is an important element in his output and his growing recognition. Close description of how the two men work on the plays. Interesting information about Wilson and the National Playwrights Center.

S057   Klein, Alvin. "Praised Dramas From State." *New York Times* 24 May 1987.
        Connecticut has supplied New York with most acclaimed dramatic offerings in season. Begins by describing *Fences* and gives a short history of appearance of the play in Connecticut. Chiefly about the fact that Wilson's plays have been seen first in Connecticut.

S058   Livingston, Dinah. "Cool August." *Minnesota Monthly* Oct. 1987: 25-32.
        Interview with Wilson in which he discusses his affection for St. Paul, his friendship with Claude Purdy, his enjoyment in writing in bars, his smoking, his past, and his poetry readings. Wilson is casual, warm, and charming in this piece. A long lively interview with cover photo of "The Bard of St. Paul." Indicates the pride St. Paul takes in his success.

S059   Mirsky, Jennifer. "The Natural Voice." *Yale Daily News Magazine* December 1987: 8-9.
        Article based on interview with Wilson in New Haven before opening of *The Piano Lesson*. Good discussion of the process of rehearsal for *The Piano Lesson* and his working relationship with Richards and the

actors. Gives Wilson's view of the new play and his attitudes about playwriting.

S060   Mordecai, Benjamin. "The August Wilson Experiment: Buying Time." *American Theatre* Jan. 1987: 26.

Discusses "production sharing" between Yale Repertory Theatre and other regional theatres as a different process than touring a play. Gives Wilson a chance to rework the play over time. Process should be an important element in development of American playwrights.

S061   Staples, Brent. "'Fences': No Barrier to Emotion." *New York Times* 5 Apr. 1987: 1.

A black writer expresses his response to *Fences*. For blacks this isn't theatre, it is life. The play exactly represents the background of many blacks attending it. The author was moved to tears, particularly by the conflict between Troy and his son: "That's exactly how it was."

S062   Witham, Barry. "Resonances of Joe Turner." Program from Seattle Repertory Theatre January 1987: 6-7.

Description of a poetry reading by Wilson and a reading of the first scene of *Fences* at the Poetry Center in New York City. Wilson discussed the real Joe Turner with the author following the reading. Witham relates Wilson's play to the historical realities of 20th-century black life in America.

1988

Reviews

R063   Barnes, Clive. "O'Neill in Blackface." *New York Post* 28 Mar. 1988. In *New York Theatre Critics' Reviews*, 1988: 320.

Compares Wilson to O'Neill in leisurely pace, control, and theatricality. *Joe Turner* is about separation which strikes a universal note. The idiom, language, and form are black and the mixture of fact and metaphor, naturalism and symbolism of play beautifully staged by Richards. Cast is excellent and carries the slowly developing play to a moving climax.

R064   Cohen, Ron. Rev. of *Joe Turner's Come and Gone*. *Women's Wear Daily* 30 Mar. 1988. In *New York Theatre Critics' Reviews*, 1988: 319.

Wilson is at crest of his power with a telling panorama of American life early in this century. Splendid performances under direction of Richards. Stunning climax occurs in this play which is evocative, as was *Fences*, but more original in scope.

R065   Kissel, Howard. "The Reunion Rag." *Daily News* 28 Mar. 1988. In *New York Theatre Critics' Reviews*, 1988: 319.

Joe Turner's Come and Gone is set in ragtime era and therefore somewhat less jazzy than two earlier plays. Wilson writes a play capturing the energy of black faith and mysticism. Could have had a little more excitement in play, but scenes of great power, particularly with Lindo as Loomis. No weak links in cast as directed by Richards.

R066   Kroll, Jack. "August Wilson's Come to Stay." *Newsweek* 11 Apr. 1988: 82.

A major writer illuminates the black experience with *Joe Turner's Come and Gone* which is his best so far and is profoundly American. Long article discusses play and Wilson's career. Indicates relationship between material in Wilson's life and the plays. Notes "unprecedented feat" for a black playwright: two plays running on Broadway.

R067   Oliver, Edith. "Boarding-House Blues." *New Yorker* 11 Apr. 1988: 107.

Joe Turner's Come and Gone is a collage of episodes and characters but with a strong narrative strain. The strange, dreamlike past encroaches on the play, but there are scenes of comedy and gaiety, particularly when the characters dance the juba. Wilson's work has its own particular quality. Excellent acting, setting, lighting, and costumes.

R068   Rich, Frank. "Panoramic History of Blacks in America in Wilson's 'Joe Turner.'" *New York Times* 28 Mar. 1988. In *New York Theatre Critics' Reviews*, 1988: 318.

A long positive review noting earlier successes and the place of the play in Wilson's cycle. Play has "occasions of true mystery and high drama" and is more impressive than in earlier work. Play is about a search for identity in the dark past. Certain weakness in overstatement of theme in long first act and characterization of children. But play is indescribably moving.

R069   Stearns, David Patrick. "'Turner' Comes to a Near Halt." *USA Today* 29 Mar. 1988. In *New York Theatre Critics' Reviews*, 1988. 323.

A windy story of alienation which never erupts. Some flashes of profundity. Character of Loomis could be anyone including a Vietnam veteran and play has some moments, but cast is "so-so." Directing is at odds with the play. Very short, negative review.

R070   Watt, Douglas. "Second Thoughts on First Nights." *Daily News* 8 Apr. 1988. In *New York Theatre Critics' Reviews*, 1988: 319.

Wilson's epic vision, power, and poetic sense lift *Joe Turner* to strange and compelling heights. People are looking for their identities and trying to find a place in the world. Cast is exceptionally well directed by Richards straight to "orgiastic climax" as striking as the stage can offer.

R071   Wilson, Edwin. "Will It Play on Broadway?" *Wall Street Journal* 18 Apr. 1988. In *New York Theatre Critics' Reviews*, 1988: 321.

Wilson explores what elements contribute to success on Broadway. *Joe Turner* succeeds because it is a powerhouse of a play with the size and scope required for Broadway. Close analysis of the theatrical qualities of the play. Concludes that Wilson is an exceptional dramatist creating a Chekhovian mosaic which builds to a volcanic eruption.

R072   Winer, Linda. "'Joe Turner' Enriches Wilson's Cycle." *New York Newsday* 28 Mar. 1988. In *New York Theater Critics' Reviews*, 1988: 323.

Scenes in the play so unexpected and unusual that one gasps. This is his best play yet, filled with strangeness. All the stories told contribute to the whole fabric of the play. Many fine performances, although a few rough around the edges. Richards and Wilson contribute richness to the theatre with the new play.

Articles, Chapters, Sections

S073   "August Wilson." *Contemporary Black Playwrights and Their Plays*. Ed. Bernard L. Peterson, Jr. New York: Greenwood, 1988: 505-6.

Short description of life and career. Discussion of plays and critical response. Describes Wilson as a "self-educated poet-playwright and director." Brief resume of his life from birth in Pittsburgh to founding of Black Horizons Theatre there, then his work with Lloyd Richards and success in New York theatre. Lists awards. Indicates *Joe Turner's Come and Gone* is a work in progress originally titled *The Mills Hand's Lunch Bucket*.

S074   Barbour, David. "August Wilson's Here to Stay." *Theater Week* 18 Apr. 1988: 8-14.

Lengthy article explores Wilson's approach to playwriting and to historical research for plays. Analysis of *Joe Turner's Come and Gone*. Joe Turner was an actual historical figure. Close consideration of themes in the plays Wilson has written so far and how they function theatrically in the plays.

S075   Bernstein, Richard. "August Wilson's Voices From the Past." *New York Times* 27 Mar. 1988: 1, 34.
            Calls *Joe Turner* Wilson's best play so far. Quotes Wilson on his development as a playwright, early difficulties, and aspirations. Discusses Wilson's plans for a cycle. Calls the plays so far "a flourishing of drama about the black identity." Wilson committed to writing plays: "This is my life."

S076   Byrne, David. "August Wilson's 'The Piano Lesson.'" *Theater* 19, 1988: 2.
            Article discusses aspects of Wilson's new play which will open at Yale Repertory Theatre. Wilson's ideas about the play, his intentions in presenting the material, view of theatre. Discussion of the continuing relationship between director Richards and playwright Wilson.

S077   Ching, Mei-Ling. "Wrestling Against History." *Theater* Summer/Fall 1988: 70-71.
            Wilson's heritage goes back to African traditions and his plays are a blend of Christianity and African cosmology. The last three of his four plays relate to those elements are are immersed in a sense of mystery. Discusses religion, ritual, prophets, and exorcism in related to those plays.

S078   Glover, E. Margaret. "The Songs of a Marked Man." *Theater* Summer/Fall 1988: 69-70.
            Talks about music, the history of black music, and the difficulty for blacks in a white man's world. The characters in *Joe Turner* take a dangerous journey and must be "consumed by the music" to find their songs. Considers the "underlying agony" between the idea that music provides freedom and the fact that music is not enough to live free.

S079   Jackson, Caroline. "Starletta DuPois: On the August
            Wilson Express." *Black Masks* Apr./May 1988: 4, 5, 13.
                    Author questions DuPois about her role in *The
            Piano Lesson*. Discussion of the characterization of
            women, implications in plays written by Wilson. Actress
            reveals attitude about the play, the process of rehearsal,
            and her view of Wilson's work.

S080   Nassour, Ellis. "The Proximity of Danger: Billy Dee
            Williams." *Theater Week* 7 Mar. 1988: 8-11.
                    Williams took over the role of Troy Maxson when
            Jones had to leave. He discusses the challenge of playing
            the role which won Jones a Tony Award. Discussion of the
            character of Troy. A short piece but interesting.

S081   Savran, David. *In Their Own Words*. New York: Theatre
            Communications Group, 1988.
                    A 1987 interview with Wilson introduced by an
            overview of his career. Author questions Wilson about his
            early career, Wilson describes first efforts at writing, work
            at Science Museum, Wilson says the most important
            experience in his training was work the O'Neill
            Playwrights Conference. Answers questions about plays,
            characters, and critics' response.

S082   Stone, Les. "August Wilson." *Contemporary Authors*, vol.
            122. Detroit: Gale, 1988: 484-485.
                    Overview of Wilson's life and his playwriting.
            Good list of the many awards he has won year by year,
            description of each of the plays in terms of action and
            character. Brief biographical material, and an analysis of
            Wilson's goals in writing.

1989

Articles, Chapters, Sections

S083   DeVries, Hilary. "The Drama of August Wilson."
        Dialogue no. 1, 1989: 48-55.
                Adapted from a 1987 article by DeVries in
        American Theatre, this is enhanced with many large color
        photographs of the plays and a photo of Wilson on the
        cover. The long article and the photographs indicate the
        increasing importance of Wilson in American theatre and
        culture.

S084   Gussow, Mel. "Fine-Tuning 'The Piano Lesson.'" *New
        York Times* 10 Sept. 1989, sec. 2: 19, 58, 60.
                Author interviews Wilson and Richards about the
        new play. Questions them about the process of playing
        around the country before coming in to New York. Wilson
        learns from staged readings and from observing the
        audiences during performances. He and Richards work
        together on final script. The play changes as it moves
        around the country.

S085   Moyers, Bill. "August Wilson's America." *American
        Theatre* June 1989: 12-17, 54-56.
                A long interview with Wilson in which Moyers
        reveals his admiration for the playwright's work. Wilson
        answers questions about his life, his views on culture and
        on theatre, his attitudes about the possibilities for blacks,
        and his general views as expressed in this interview for the
        PBS series "A World of Ideas."

S086   Moyers, Bill. Interview with August Wilson. *A World of
        Ideas*. New York: Doubleday, 1989.
                Essentially the same material as S085 which was
        the result of the interview for the PBS series "A World of
        Ideas."

S087   O'Neill, Michael C. "August Wilson." *American Playwrights Since 1945*. New York: Greenwood, 1989: 512-27.

             Lists awards Wilson has won and a picture of his career to date. Thorough coverage gives a production history of his plays with a critical response to each. List sources for resarch on Wilson, bibliography, and future research opportunities on a playwright developing into a major figure in American theatre.

S088   Shafer, Yvonne. "An Interview with August Wilson." *Journal of Dramatic Theory and Criticism* Fall 1989: 161-174.

             Wilson answers questions about early life, scripts for the Science Museum, his attitude toward playwriting, how he actually creates characters, gives a long discussion of the genesis of forthcoming *Two Trains Running,* and his own habit of writing in diners and coffee houses. Wilson is warm and forthcoming in discussing his background and his attitude toward theatre.

S089   Shannon, Sandra G. "The Good Christian's Come and Gone: The Shifting Role of Christianity in August Wilson Plays." *Melus* Fall 1989-90: 127-142.

             African American men are the center of Wilson's plays and are related to the abandonment of Christianity. Discusses the role of Christianity in black history in America. Notes that for Troy Maxson Christianity plays no role, Loomis has "disgust for the deity," and Boy Willie mocks religion. In contrast to the Biblical Job, they have given up on God.

1990-1997

1990

Reviews

R090   Barnes, Clive. "'Piano Lesson' Hits All the Right Keys."
                New York Post 17 Apr. 1990. In *New York Theatre
                Critics' Reviews,* 1990: 325-26.
                     Praises all aspects saying the wonderful Pulitzer
                Prize winner is magnificent. Best and most immediate of
                all his plays. Wilson is most acclaimed playwright of his
                time. Compares with Shakespeare in his feel for human
                nature. Notes comedy. Best ensemble playing on
                Broadway.

R091   Beaufort, John. "Wilson Renews His Look at Black Life."
                Christian Science Monitor 23 Apr. 1990. In *New York
                Theatre Critics' Reviews,* 1990: 327.
                     The Piano Lesson reconfirms Wilson's major
                status as a playwright. Seeming digressions are really part
                of the total human fabric of remarkable play. Dutton
                energizes whole production in dynamic and comic role.
                Theatrically superb ending exciting, play is momentous
                theatrical occasion.

R092   Kissel, Howard. "A Bitter 'Lesson.'" *Daily News* 17 Apr.
                1990. In *New York Theatre Critics' Reviews,* 1990: 324.
                     The story of the family struggle over the piano is
                fascinating. Many moments don't advance central story
                but are engrossing because of Wilson's ability with
                language. Felt characters could have been more deeply
                analyzed. Although Wilson hasn't quite succeeded in his
                attempt to combine realism and mysticism, play is
                important because may help push American theatre
                beyond petty naturalism.

R093   Kelly, Kevin. "Heart and Mind Are in Right Place in 'Two
                Trains Running.'" *Boston Globe* 5 Apr. 1990.

Premiere of play at Yale Rep. Although nothing is extraneous, there is a lack of definition in the play. Its heart and mind are in the right place and it is Wilson's easiest and most natural play, but it is short on definition. Cast and direction are wonderful. Problems are corrrectable with Richards/Wilson collaboration.

R094   Kramer, Mimi. "Travelling Man and Hesitating Woman." *New Yorker* 30 Apr. 1990: 82-83.

Discusses the setting and the visual qualities of *The Piano Lesson*. Dutton's performance starts too high and becomes tiresome. Play needs cutting, ending is mystical and melodramatic. Ending and message of play are obscure because playwright raises questions which are not answered.

R095   Kroll, Jack. Review of *The Piano Lesson*. *Newsweek* 19 Feb. 1990. In *New York Theatre Critics' Reviews*, 1990: 329.

Wilson carries the day with emotional power, tragic and comic eloquence and sense of history with bloodstained ghosts yet to be exorcised. Praises Richards, cast, especially Dutton. Playing at UCLA theatre before New York opening, packing the audiences in. But too long for him--suggests Wilson should cut before moving on.

R096   Rich, Frank. "A Family's Past in Wilson's 'Piano Lesson.'" *New York Times* 17 Apr. 1990: 1B, 2B.

Notes that the play won the Pulitzer Prize. It is a joyously African-American play which bubbles and thunders for three hours. Symbol of the piano significant in play's theme of the past and slavery. Dutton a rare actor, cast excellent. No white characters but presence of white America felt. Music in the play belongs to the characters, "it is not for sale."

R097   Spillane, Margaret. "Pulitzered Piano, Trying-Out Trains." *Theater Week* 7 May 1990: 37-38.

Wilson's plays brave in treatment of poor African Americans. Astonishing moments in *The Piano Lesson*. Discusses improvements in addition of music and altered ending since performance at Yale Repertory Theatre. Ending still problematic. Women not as interesting as men in Wilson's work. But calls play a fine ghost story. Also reviews *Two Trains Running* which opened at Yale Repertory. Discusses the background of the 1960s, notes it does not figure much in the play. Ending unsatisfactory, but play is important.

R098   Stearns, David Patrick. "'The Piano Lesson" Heavy on Drills." *USA Today* 17 Apr. 1990. In *New York Theatre Critics Reviews*, 1990: 326.

Won Pulitzer Prize four days before New York opening and needs it because doesn't feel play will attract audiences. Easy to respect, but not to enjoy. Dutton is obnoxious as Boy Willie. Some scenes most compelling Wilson has written. Performances are Tony Award quality. Brief, peculiarly mixed review.

R099   "'Two Trains Running' Is Not Quite On Track." *Hartford Courant* 9 April 1990: 9A, 11A.

Play premiering at Yale Rep is not ready to begin presentations across country. Wilson's powers of dialogue and characterizations present, but play never arrives at its destination. Thinks playwright and director Richards divided efforts between this and *Piano Lesson*. Direction is not satisfactory.

R100   Watt, Douglas. "Star Key to 'Piano Lesson.'" *Daily News* 20 Apr. 1990. In *New York Theatre Critics Reviews*, 1990: 324.

Dutton's name properly above title because his dynamic performance almost draws together the diffuse, Chekhovian play. Wilson has not created a successful total text. In particular, ending is questionable. In many ways a masterly composition, but not fully devised.

R101   Wilson, David. "A Train to Catch." *New Haven Advocate*
            9 Apr. 1990.
                   Finds Wilson at his best in world premiere at Yale
            Rep. Long review says it is clearly a work in progress, but
            is joyous, exhilarating, and funny. Despite its flaws, a
            stunning play you must not miss. Discussion of many
            metaphors. Ending is anti-climactic and play is too
            episodic. Directing is excellent, cast talented, play will
            probably be a worthy successor to earlier Wilson work.

R102   Wilson, Edwin. "Theater: A Lesson in Life." *Wall Street
            Journal* 18 Dec. 1987. In *New York Theatre Critics
            Reviews*, 1990: 328.
                   Lesson is that blacks are often deprived of
            symbols of the past and opportunity in the present. Wilson
            has sure instinct for drama, unfailing ear for rich verbal
            lore. First class farce and fine serious scenes. *The Piano
            Lesson* is at Yale Rep and will have rewrites. Needs
            cutting, but Wilson can fix what is wrong so play will take
            place with other remarkable works in cycle.

R103   Wilson, Edwin. "August Wilson's 'The Piano Lesson.'"
            Wall Street Journal 23 Apr. 1990. In *New York Theatre
            Critics Reviews*, 1990: 328.
                   After more than two years of performing it is
            essentially the same with strengths and a few weaknesses.
            Dutton mesmerizing and charming as Boy Willie. Wilson
            better than other playwrights in scenes of confrontation,
            tender love scenes, comical love scenes created with
            authority and stage magic. Still too long and ghost at end
            is problematic.

R104   Winer, Linda. "August Wilson's Haunting 'Piano
            Lesson.'" *New York Newsday* 17 Apr. 1990. In *New York
            Theatre Critics Reviews*, 1990: 328.
                   Special vision and rich characters in Wilson's
            plays. Lovely tragi-comedy, haunting as well as haunted.
            Ending is deus ex machina which doesn't answer questions

raised. But effect of play and dialogue remains long after play is over. Dutton spectacular, others excellent.

Articles, Chapters, Sections

S105   Brustein, Robert. "The Lesson of 'The Piano Lesson.'" *New Republic* 21 May 1990: 28-30.
            Beginning of a major dispute over Wilson, black theatre, and the role of non-profit theatres. Objects to Yale and other resident theatres as launching pads for Broadway plays. Calls Wilson's new play "overwritten exercise in conventional style" with little power or poetry. Use of supernatural is poor playwriting. Richards at fault for not insisting on cuts. Says only proper to compare Wilson to O'Neill because of shared faults, and like O'Neill was too highly praised for weak early work. Richards has inappropriately spent time away from Yale working with Wilson.

S106   Brustein, Robert. Reply to letters attacking above article. *New Republic* 18 June 1990: 3.
            Author defends his point of view and denies saying Wilson should not continue writing about black people, because his themes and style are repetitious.

S107   Greene, Alexis. "Charles S. Dutton: Not Ready to Accept Defeat." *Theater Week* 18 June 1990: 36-39.
            Author questions dynamic, exciting actor Dutton about performing in Wilson plays. Discusses his emotional and intuitive response to the roles, particularly the latest (Dutton's favorite), Boy Willie in *The Piano Lesson*. Actor talks about rehearsals and work with Wilson developing characters in the plays.

S108   Jackson, Caroline. "'The Piano Lesson': A Chronicle Continued." *Black Masks* Oct./Nov. 1990: 8, 9, 21.
            Dutton's work from first Wilson play in New York to the latest is the center of this consideration of the actors who play the demanding roles in "The Piano Lesson." The

play began in New Haven and has had a long pre-Broadway tour. Dutton has been praised for the sensational performance of the dialogue Wilson has written.

S109   Kaminker, Laura. "Letter to Editor." *New Republic* 18 June 1990: 2.

        Response to Brustein's article from a white person who finds the attack on Wilson unacceptable. Says white people don't go to the plays because of guilt but because they identify with the plays.

S110   Moyers, Bill. "Africa's Spirit." *Utne Reader* Mar./Apr. 1990: 105.

        A short excerpt from S085. Focus on Wilson's view that there is nothing wrong with black culture as opposed, say, to Japanese, it is just different.

S111   Rich, Frank. "Broadway's Bounty: Dramas Brimming With Life." *New York Times* 3 June 1990, sec. 2: 1, 8.

        Overview of the season on the day of the Tony Awards. Calls *Piano Lesson* one of the "more exhilirating treats." Notes that three of the nominated plays began in non-profit theatres and calls them adventurous works. As a playwright Wilson is introducing white audiences to black America without patronizing either.

S112   Rothstein, Mervyn. "The Tony vs. the Pulitzers." *New York Times* 3 June 1990, sec. 2: 8.

        Brief article about Wilson's chance to win the Tony. *Piano Lesson* won the Pulitzer Prize and has a chance for the Tony tonight. Gives a brief list of winners of both prizes which did not go on to win the Tony.

S113   Rothstein, Mervyn. "Passionate Beliefs Renew Theater Fight Over Art and Profit." *New York Times* 15 May 1990: C13.

        Describes the dispute aroused by Brustein's articles and comments about Wilson and Richards. Photos of Brustein and Richards who hold conflicting points of view about Wilson and the role of resident theatres. Quotes from people on both sides. Brustein says it is wrong to say he has a personal vendetta. Richards declined to comment.

S114   "Two-Timer." *Time* 23 Apr. 1990: 99.
              Wilson is one of only seven dramatists to win two Pulitzer Prizes. Second is for *Piano Lesson* which is quite different from *Two Trains*, the only similarity being that they are both terrific. Brief piece essentially pointing out Wilson's accomplishment.

S115   Vaughan, Peter. "St. Paul Dramatist's Award Is His Second." *Mineapolis Star Tribune* 13 Apr. 1990: 1A, 14A.
              Wilson is informed while in a coffee shop of second Pulitzer Prize. He feels *The Piano Lesson* deals with larger issues than *Fences* Wilson is inspired to go to work immediately on new play. Articles treats Wilson's career with focus on St. Paul and notes many local careers were bolstered because of work with Wilson.

S116   Viertel, Jack. "Letter to Editor." *New Republic* 18 June 1990: 3.
              Says Brustein's article reveals he is lost in an ivory tower unaware of realities of theatre today. Defends *Piano Lesson* saying it is certainly no commercial vehicle and that institutional theatres should continue to produce such plays because they can't get started on Broadway.

1991

Articles, Chapters, Sections

S117   DeVries, Hilary. "Theater's Godfather Reaches Entr'acte." *New York Times* 30 June 1991, sec. 2: 1.

Appreciation of Lloyd Richards' role in American theatre as he takes a reluctant leave after twelve years as Dean of Yale School of Drama. Discusses his work with playwrights including Hansberry and Fugard. Calls work with Wilson "one of the most significant director-playwright relationships in modern theatre." Notes that Richards was sometimes criticized for static direction of the plays and not insisting that they be cut more.

S118   Harrison, Paul Carter. "August Wilson's Blues Poetics." in Wilson's *Three Plays*. Pittsburgh: University of Pittsburgh, 1991: 291-318.

Wilson's cycle is hewn from bedrock of racial memory. Gives view of history of black music and culture, relating them to Wilson's plays. Analyses of Wilson's first three plays particularly in terms of the importance of music in the plays and to individual characters. Description of importance of particular characters in relation to history.

S119   Shafer, Yvonne. "August Wilson: A New Approach to Black Drama." *Zeitschrift für Änglistik und Amerikanistik* 1, 1991: 17-27.

Wilson's plays have attracted white audiences as well as blacks. Discusses his success in the theatre and examines his first four plays in terms of character and themes. Thorough discussion of critical and popular reaction to Wilson's plays up to this time. Considers Wilson's position in the American theatre. Contains material from an interview with Wilson in which he discusses his views about playwriting and the process he follows.

S120   Shannon, Sandra G. "From Lorraine Hansberry to August Wilson." *Callaloo* Winter 1991: 124-135.

A long interview with Lloyd Richards preceded by a brief description of his career. Describes work with Wilson starting with revisions of initial *Ma Rainey* to final version. Richards answers questions regarding the ending of *Piano Lesson*, significance of female characters in the plays, Wilson's effect on the American theatre, response of white audiences to his plays, use of light, and the use of music.

S121   Shannon, Sandra G. "The Long Wait: August Wilson's *Ma Rainey's Black Bottom*." *Black American Literature Forum* Spring 1991: 136-146.

Themes of waiting in the play relate to black history. The musicians are always practicing and waiting and the audience shares the experience of waiting. Discussion of the real Ma Rainey and the character in the play. Focuses on the waiting of blacks which frustrates them and stifles their talents.

S122   Wilde, Lisa. "Reclaiming the Past: Narrative and Memory in August Wilson's *Two Trains Running*." *Theater* Winter 1990-91: 73-74.

Discussion of the new play. Characters need to reclaim what has been lost or stolen. The liberating moments in Wilson's plays come from communicating "with supernatural or occult mysteries." Wilson and Richards have recovered their own personal histories through collaboration and in the plays "memory has been given a voice."

1992

Reviews

R123   Ansen, David. "Of Prophets and Profits." *Newsweek* 27 Apr. 1992. In *New York Theatre Critics' Reviews*, 1992: 141.

Wilson presents *Two Trains Running* which is not about the '60s but a series of stories behind politics from which the audience can learn about the '60s. Discusses the characters and calls the play thematically rich. It is a series of "street-wise arias and monologues" rising to eloquence. Impressively acted and directed.

R124   Barnes, Clive. "'Trains' Doesn't Run." *New York Post* 14
              Apr. 1992. In *New York Theatre Critics' Reviews*, 1992:
              138.
                    Most diffuse play Wilson has written. Discusses
              the theme of life and death. Nothing much happens in long
              three-hour play. Staging is self-conscious although acting
              is excellent. Play lacks focus and immediacy, too much
              padding. Says white audiences will look for more
              edification and immediacy than the play gives. There are
              some scenes of vivid stage life.

R125   Beaufort, John. "Wilson's 'Two Trains Running' Scores."
              Christian Science Monitor 28 Apr. 1992. In *New York
              Theatre Critics' Reviews*, 1992: 140.
                    The play should add to Wilson's laurels.
              Describes the play as a human collage of fragments which
              are funny, touching, and gripping. Moves slowly to come
              together, but the author is in control of playwriting
              technique. First-rate cast and director. This is the most
              comic play Wilson has written: the humor is in the speech
              patterns and oddities of language, not gags. Fine setting
              and costumes. Predicts a long run.

R126   Henry III, William A. "Luncheonette Tone Poem." *Time*
              27 Apr. 1992. In *New York Theatre Critics' Reviews*,
              1992: 142.
                    Notes that Wilson was a poet before turning to
              plays and more sensitive to "metaphors than manifestos."
              Says Wilson is at his lyrical best in this remarkable play
              which is his most delicate and mature work. It covers a
              whole range of political, social, and philosophical
              questions regarding black people under the guise of a slice
              of life. Roscoe Lee Browne plays the showiest role
              beautifully, but all the actors are superb.

R127   Kissel, Howard. "'Trains': The Tales of August." *Daily
              News* 14 Apr. 1992. In *New York Theatre Critics'
              Reviews*, 1992: 137.

Some of the strongest moments in Wilson's plays are those in which people simply tell stories, particularly in this latest play in which there is almost no action. Wilson has a gift for capturing rhythms and charm of black speech with a musical quality. Says a few '60s references, but could be in any era. Play has weaknesses, but there is great strength in the cast, especially Browne and Fishburne. Play carefully "orchestrated" by Richards.

R128   Rich, Frank. "August Wilson Reaches the '60s with Witnesses from a Distance." *New York Times* 14 Apr. 1992. In *New York Theatre Critics' Reviews*, 1992: 139.

Rich likes *Two Trains Running* better than the production and writes a long appreciative review. It treats the headlines of the '60s through the depiction or ordinary characters removed from major events. The glorious language is the fiber of the play which has little plot. The play deals with the choices blacks make between different types of prophets. But the play is flawed in the unfulfilled characterizations of Risa and Sterling. Browne and Fishburne are excellent, but the others only adequate. Production seems tired from the long tour, has inappropriate set and lighting, and is directed contrary to the script. Nevertheless, the play is fascinating and indirectly captures the period.

R129   Richards, David. "A People Face the Mirror of History." *New York Times* 3 May 1992, Sec. 2: 5.

Says *Two Trains Running* is surprising because it is not an explosive exploration of an explosive period. It is Wilson's most benevolent and funny play and is "Saroyanesque." Discusses the themes and stories. Appreciates excellent language and fine acting which prevent the play from seeming amorphous. Thinks that the fact that the play doesn't "go" anywhere is a comment on the '60s which changed very little in society in the end. But the play's "poetic vitality" is a rejection of hopelessness.

R130   Simon, John. Rev. *Two Trains Running*. *New York Magazine* 27 Apr. 1992: 135.

Describes symbolism of play and says is a step forward in Wilson's stagecraft. Does not rely on obvious dramatics. Says it is a play of inner action with interesting characters. Play, staging, acting attain the necessary theatrical truth. Some negative criticism of Richards' direction.

R131   Stearns, David Patrick. "Wilson's 'Trains' on Track." *USA Today* 14 Apr. 1992. In *New York Theatre Critics' Reviews*, 1992: 142.

Short but appreciative review says Wilson has a loyal following and new play will convert more. This is his most moving play, well-focused and mingles comedy and tragedy with breathtaking elegance. Calls Risa the emotional center of the play; acting is consistently great, play is among the best this season, thanks to Richards' direction.

R132   Watt, Douglas. "Colorful Characters Keep 'Two Trains Running.'" *Daily News* 24 Apr. 1992. In *New York Theatre Critics' Reviews*, 1992: 137.

Describes the interesting characters which make an interesting evening in the theatre. Calls it a plotless play, but happy, and although the parts never really cohere, there are fine performances, Wilson's voice is continually interesting, and the evening is never dull.

R133   Wilson, Edwin. Rev. *Two Trains Running*. *Wall Street Journal* 20 Apr. 1992. In *New York Theatre Critics' Reviews*, 1992: 141.

Calls Wilson the outstanding American playwright of the past decade. However, feels in this production the audience must be satisfied with Wilson's unfailing talent for dialogue, storytelling, and his golden language because the play lacks a major, unifying struggle to give it focus and move it forward.

R134   Winer, Linda. "Grappling with Their Stations in Life."
            New York Newsday 14 Apr. 1992. In *New York Theatre
            Critics' Reviews*, 1992: 136.
                    Winer, who voted for *Two Trains Running* to win
            the New York Drama Critics Circle Award, praises the
            play while admitting that some theatregoers may find it
            long. Says in his five plays Wilson has populated the
            century with people we otherwise would not have met and
            who refuse to be forgotten. Roles for actors to love, fine
            acting and directing.

                          Articles, Chapters, Sections

S135   Bigsby, C.W.E. *Modern American Drama, 1945-1990.*
            Cambridge: Cambridge U. Press, 1992. 285-298.
                    Short section on Wilson's life and career precedes
            detailed analyses of plays from *Ma Rainey's Black Bottom*
            through *Joe Turner's Come and Gone.* Notes "the past is
            the present" in Wilson's plays. Observes that many of the
            plays were the first by a black playwright to be performed
            in some American regional theatres.

S136   Johnson, Malcolm. "Murphy: Time Is Not on His Side in
            'Fences.'" *Hartford Courant* 3 Dec. 1992: 9.
                    Relates to the controversy over filming *Fences*
            with the script Wilson has written. Eddie Murphy and
            Paramount bought the rights to the film, but controversy
            over the director has stalled production. Now Murphy,
            who was to play the teenage son, is turning 32 and it may
            be too late. Wilson wants a black director for the film.

S137   McKelly, James C. "Hymns of Sedition: Portraits of the
            Artist in Contemporary African-American Drama."
            Arizona Quarterly Spring 1992: 87-107.
                    Article covers wide range of plays including
            Raisin in the Sun and Baraka's *The Slave.* Last section is
            good, close, lengthy analysis of *Ma Rainey.* Considers
            social and psychological tension of the '20s reflected in
            the play. Contrasts characters in conflict, focusing on Ma

Rainey and Levee. He is viewed as a "product of new socioeconomic possibilities." As a "levee" he fails to hold back the forces pushing him.

S138   Miller, Russell. "On a Napkin in a Coffee Shop, Life Is Written (A Play, Too)." *New York Times* 3 June 1992: 1C.
        Article about Wilson who is rehearsing *Two Trains* in New York. Talks about his haircuts, pleasure in writing in coffee shops and drinking lots of coffee, writing on napkins, his love for the blues, and reveals his propensity as a storyteller. Nice picture of Wilson's easygoing charm and his views about life and theatre.

S139   Ruling, Karl G. "Christopher Akerlind." *Theatre Crafts* Jan. 1992: 35, 54.
        Interview with the lighting designer for *The Piano Lesson*. Discussion of the importance of lighting in the play, particularly in connection with the supernatural elements and the ending. Questions about the changes in the play from Yale Rep premiere through long tour.

S140   Vaughan, Peter. "Purdy Has Long Admired Man He Portrays in 'Malcolm X' at Walker." *Minneapolis Star Tribune* 29 Nov. 1992: 8F.
        Article based on an interview with Lester Purdy who is performing in Minneapolis in a one-man play written by August Wilson. Play was written in 1980 for Lou Bellamy, artistic director of Penumbra Theatre. New production is at the Walker Art Center.

S141   Weeks, Jerome. "August Wilson Sings the Blues." *Dallas Morning News* 18 Oct. 1992: 1C.
        Article based on interview with Wilson. Author says each of Wilson's plays finds a force at odds with black self-determination. He notes Wilson's position as a playwright who has won two Pulitzer Prizes. Talks about Wilson's inspiration from music and the importance of the blues to black people and notes impact of music in all of

his plays. Discussion of new play *Seven Guitars*. Long quotes from Wilson about meaning in his plays and future plans.

S142   Wontorek, Paul. "Respect." *Theater Week* 27 July 1992: 10-13.

Article based on interview with Larry Fishburne who was given the Tony Award for his performance in *Two Trains*. He has fulfilled two dreams: to originate a role on Broadway and to work with August Wilson. In no hurry to leave the play as it is "serious drama about black people on the great *white*way."

1993

Reviews

R143   Billington, Michael. "Family Discord." *The Guardian* 9 October 1993: n.p.

Says *The Piano Lesson* at the Tricycle Theatre in London is flawed in that it is too long and has a mystical, melodramatic ending, but that the evening is engrossing and he felt there was something momentous at stake. Wilson is compared favorably to O'Neill and Ibsen in using the past to inform the present. A family dispute becomes a powerful social metaphor. The domestic and social blend in a play "about the need to acknowledge the past without being in thrall to it."

R144   Blanchard, Jayne M. "This 'Piano' Found the Key for Great Theater." *St. Paul Pioneer Press* 8 May 1993: 5C.

Powerful play and powerful production of *The Piano Lesson* at Penumbra. Fine acting and directing by Marion Isaac McClinton make the play funnier, sexier and more abandoned than New York production. The play is three and a half hours long but wholly engaging all the time.

R145   Christiansen, Richard. "'Piano Lesson' Is Back in Session." *Chicago Tribune* 20 Jan. 1993: 20.

Review of a revival of the play which was seen at the Goodman in Chicago before the New York premiere. The strengths of the play are clear, but the "hocus-pocus" ending doesn't satisfy audience and probably not the playwright. Language is "beguiling, evocative, and powerful." Direction by Steven Billington is a little too vigorous. Actors are effective in production at Illinois Theatre Center.

R146   Christiansen, Richard. "'Two Trains' Has Ticket to Amazing Trip." *Chicago Tribune* 26 Jan 1993: 16.

Calls Wilson's cycle of dramas extraordinary. Strong praise for the language which gives each of the actors lyric moments. Finds rich themes in the play, suggests the ultimate meaning is that before a new age can begin "the leaders of the future have to square things with the past." Play at the Goodman is not strident, but funny and casual. Outstanding, sensitive direction by Richards. Characters are small people but they "summon up a universe."

R147   Frazin, Julian. "'Two Trains' Runs Faster than an Alley Cat and a Cockroach." *Chicago Lawyer* March 1993: 73.

Notes that the production follows three earlier successes with Wilson plays at the Goodman Theatre. Richards' direction is sensitive and the cast is brilliant. In contrast to the movies of Spike Lee no rage or violence. Wilson shows little people who survive life's calamities and says there are two trains running and one can choose life rather than death and live with dignity.

R148   Morley, Sheridan. "'The Piano Lesson' Explores the Legacy of Slavery." *International Herald Tribune* 13 October 1993.

Implies that Wilson is treated with too much reverence on Broadway because his plays are politically correct. It is better to see them abroad as in present production at the Tricycle Theatre. The play is about an hour too long and the ending is laughable. Director Paulette Randall does her best to "haul Wilson into the league of O'Casey and O'Neill."

R149   Patner, Andrew. "'Piano Lesson,' 'Trains' Provide Wilson Bonanza." *Chicago Sun-Times* 28 Jan. 1993, Sec. 2: 35.

Rare opportunity to see two excellent productions of Wilson plays in Chicago. Goodman has been tryout and tour host for Wilson's work, has excellent *Two Trains Running*. Now smaller, lower budget Illinois Theatre Center shows it can also be successful with playwright's work. Calls *Piano Lesson* a panoramic work of family conflict, but says Wilson still doesn't know how to end it. Praise for actors.

R150   Taylor, Paul. "Family Plot." *The Independent* 9 Oct. 1993: 30.

Praises Wilson for his creation of a cycle of plays, "a long and rich work-in-progress." Says unfortunate to group with Neil Simon as Wilson is superior. London *Piano Lesson* is beautifully acted at the Tricycle Theatre. Wilson shows the difficulty of paying reverence to the sufferings of the past and going on. Finds the ending too literal, but the play as a whole attractive because it is so large-minded and warm-spirited.

R151   Vaughan, Peter. "'Piano Lesson' Gets a Clear, Well-acted Staging." *Minneapolis Star Tribune* 7 May 1993: 14E, 15E.

This is perhaps Wilson's richest play presented in a forceful and funny production. Good analysis of the themes and metaphors. Says ghosts are a constant presence and must be exorcised. Play deserved the Pulitzer Prize. Penumbra Company is very fine.

R152   Weiss, Hedy. "Wilson, Goodman Deliver Terrific 'Two Trains.'" *Chicago Sun-Times* 26 Jan. 1993, Sec. 2: 21.

Calls Wilson a truly great playwright and says the production is phenomenal. Brilliant language illuminates the past and is also a call to the future. Flawless direction by Richards. When the play ends, the audience is reluctant to say goodbye to the appealing characters.

Articles, Chapters, Sections

S153   Anderson, Addell A. "August Wilson." *Contemporary Dramatists*. Washington: St. James Press, 1993: 717-719.
Significant dates in Wilson's life and career, awards. Quotes Wilson's desire to write about the black experience in America as well as things common to all cultures. Wilson is one of America's most significant playwrights. Discusses themes, characterization, language, and visual elements in his first four plays. There is a quote by Wilson regarding his exploration of the black experience in America and his effort to "concretize the values of the black American and place them on stage."

S154   Plum, Jay. "Blues, History, and the Dramaturgy of August Wilson." *African American Review* Winter 1993: 561-567.
Discusses definitions of the blues and Wilson's aesthetic. Close analysis of some of the songs and long speeches in Wilson's plays, use of the metaphor of stew and African-Americans as leftovers. Quotes reviews and articles regarding several plays. Like the blues, Wilson's plays appeal to whites and blacks.

S155   Shannon, Sandra G. "Blues, History, and Dramaturgy." *African American Review* Winter 1993: 539-559.
Interviewer says Wilson's answers show he believes a playwright cannot follow a dictated agenda, writing poetry has shaped his work, black directors can fully appreciate the culture depicted in his plays. Good discussion of earlier works now abandoned by Wilson,

close analysis of characterization in *Two Trains Running*, Wilson's opinions about other writers and society.

S156   Vaughan, Peter. "After Three-Year Break from Writing, Wilson Ready to Finish 'Seven Guitars.'" *Minneapolis Star Tribune* 30 Apr. 1993: 1E-2E.

Telephone interview with Wilson, now living in Seattle. Discusses changes in his life and his view of *The Piano Lesson* in rehearsal both in Seattle and St. Paul. Wilson says he appreciates the play more than before and liked seeing the Seattle rehearsal. Interviewer notes gap in production of Wilson's writing, his divorce, and that he quit smoking cold turkey, and that he plans to marry costumer Constanza Romero.

1994

Reviews

R157   Blanchard, Jayne M. "'Trains' Stay Right on Track." *St. Paul Pioneer Press* 7 May 1994.

Despite length of 3 and 1/2 hours, viewer wishes for one more story, please. Play is filled with wonderful words and interesting characters. Penumbra cast is as polished and simpatico as if the actors had known each other all their lives.

R158   Simons, Tad. "Rail Life." *Twin Cities Reader* 17 May 1994: 22.

Says *Two Trains Running* runs three hours, but one would like it to go on forever. Play and Penumbra production add up to incredible theatre and take you on a journey you will never forget. Not much happens in the play and little is made of politics, but reviewer approves of all aspects.

Articles, Chapters, Sections

S159   "August Wilson." *Contemporary Authors*, Vol. 42. Detroit: Gale, 1994. 477-479.
            Production history of plays through *Two Trains Running*. Brief description of Wilson's life. Says he describes himself as a cultural nationalist. Long description of *Ma Rainey's Black Bottom*, briefer descriptions of later plays. Survey of critics' views of the plays.

S160   "August Wilson's 'Two Trains Running' Featured at the Penumbra." *Minneapolis Spokesman* 28 Apr. 1994: 1A, 8A.
            Says Minnesota's only black professional theatre company will present Wilson's play which takes a searing look at the most turbulent decade of this century. The play reveals Wilson's remarkable blend of the real and the poetic. Wilson validates the African American experience by portraying it in his plays.

S161   Bogumil, M. L. "'Tomorrow Never Comes' Songs of Cultural Identity in August Wilson's *Joe Turner's Come and Gone.*" *Theatre Journal* Dec. 1994: 463-76.
            Presents a lengthy analysis of the actual events which form the background of the play and how the characters relate to them, the importance of the Juba dance and the use of the blues. Concludes the ending shows people can change and shake off the identity as a non-man. Good discussion of the word "mark" as a theme in the play.

S162   Harris, Andrew B. *Broadway Theatre*. New York: Routledge, 1994. 126-27.
            Discussion of Wilson's approach to writing as illustrated by production of *Fences*. Says language beautifully crafted, plays move beyond realism as did Ibsen's late plays, but go farther. Young and racially mixed

audiences flock to see Wilson's plays. Not an in-depth piece, but represents a significant critic's view.

S163   "Two Trains Running." *Penumbra Theatre Company News* Spring/Summer 1994: 1-2.
Interview with Director Lou Bellamy before production of Wilson's most recent play. Praise for his work and a discussion of the value of his plays for the theatre and for the St. Paul community. Wilson says Penumbra can do his work like no other theatre because of long ties. Wilson now lives in Seattle but is still a member of the theatre.

S164   Vaughan, Peter. "Almost Played Out, Penumbra Looks to Keep Link With Wilson." *Minneapolis Star Tribune* 1 May 1994: 1F, 5F.
Article notes long connection between Wilson and theatre, but *Two Trains Running* is the last of Wilson's plays which they have not staged. Wilson has been a big draw for the theatre with extended runs of his plays. Gives figures on attendance: "The Piano Lesson" ran 10 weeks and drew 11,500 viewers. Gives director Bellamy's appreciation of Wilson, "the jewel in our crown."

Book-Length Studies

S165   Elkins, Marilyn, ed. *August Wilson: A Casebook.* New York: Garland, 1994.
Introduction by Elkins gives brief picture of Wilson's career, describes the ten essays in the book, which include political, mythical, and regional interpretations, plus gender based views and interviews with Richards and Wilson. Although essays are of uneven value, as a whole the book provides a wide range of insights.

S166   Nadel, Alan. *May All Your Fences Have Gates.* Iowa City: U. of Iowa Press, 1994.

Book of essays about Wilson providing information and insights about his plays to date. Authors treat use of jazz, history, metaphor, traditions of African performance, his characterization of women, and his insistence on a black director. Varied approaches offer a wide range of information and analysis. Annotated bibliography.

1995

Reviews

R167   Abarbanel, Jonathan. Rev. of *Seven Guitars*. *Back Stage* 10 Feb. 1995: 19.

Splendid world premiere at Goodman Theatre shows typical strength and weakness of Wilson's writing. Character-driven, not plot-driven, deep, true characters, wonderful dialogue, musical quality in play. But too much talk, play is more than three hours long. Guitar player killed by Marcus Garvey follower. Images of blood and violent death. Walter Dallas took over directing when Richards was hospitalized.

R168   "Charles Dutton, Alfre Woodard Star in TV Production of 'The Piano Lesson.'" *Jet* 30 Jan. 1995: 63.

Charles Dutton plays role of Willie Boy as in original production. Special Hallmark Hall of Fame on CBS, play cut to fit two-hour format. Directed by Lloyd Richards. Has a stellar ensemble cast. Brief description of story.

R169   Droesch, Paul. Rev. of *The Piano Lesson*. *TV Guide* 30 Jan. 1995: 43.

Lists cast of television production and director, says excellent, gives it a grade of A. Very brief.

R170   Kroll, Jack. Rev. of *Seven Guitars*. *Newsweek* 6 Feb. 1995: 60.

Party for Wilson followed premiere at famous blues club, appropriate to play and Wilson's career. No black playwright has entered the mainstream as fully as Wilson. New play set in the 1940s, supposed to tour to Boston, later to open in New York. Structure involves a death and flashbacks in a kind of jazz cantata with characters singing the blues when just talking. Wonderful production with excellent actors portraying tragic characters.

R171   Taylor, Jonathon. Rev. of *The Piano Lesson*. *Variety* 30 Jan. 1995: 41.

Production is to be on television. Lists cast, many of which were in original production in New York and have since performed together on a television series. Richards directs. Production rates an A. Brief notice.

R172   Tynan, William. "Death and the Blues." *Time* 20 Feb. 1995: 71-72.

Largely positive review of new play premiering at Goodman Theater in Chicago. Notes cast so good that flaws in the play show up. Wilson has history of rewriting plays before bringing into New York and author believes he will find its problems and solve them. Play concerns death of a guitar player named Floyd, but has too much mysticism. Directed by Walter Dallas in flawless production.

Articles, Chapters, Sections

S173   Shafer, Yvonne. "Breaking Barriers: August Wilson." *Staging Difference: Cultural Pluralism in American Theatre and Drama,* ed. Marc Maufort. New York: Peter Lang, 1995. 267-285.

Explores Wilson's career with analysis of the plays and critics' response. Comparisons to O'Neill examined. Considers Wilson's appeal to white audiences and universality of his plays. Discussion of Wilson's attitudes toward theatre and toward his work. Appraisal of his place in American theatre at this time.

Book-Length Studies

S174   Pereira, Kim. *August Wilson and the African-American Odyssey.* Chicago: U. of Illinois Press, 1995.
Develops a picture of the history of blacks in America, the development of black culture and of the blues. Analyzes plays from *Ma Rainey's Black Bottom* to *The Piano Lesson*, placing them within this perspective. Makes use of books about cultural history and folk beliefs.

S175   Shannon, Sandra G. *The Dramatic Vision of August Wilson.* Washington, DC: Howard UP, 1995.
The book includes a chronology and close analyses of Wilson's plays. The author has followed Wilson's career closely and she presents material about his life and career which affects the plays. The appendix has a long 1991 interview with Wilson conducted by the author.

1996

Reviews

R176   Armstrong, Linda. "'Joe Turner's Come and Gone' opens at the Henry Street." New York *Amsterdam News* 26 Oct. 1996: 25.
Reviewer recently saw *Seven Guitars* which was magnificent. This play not as neatly packaged and takes some time for theme of what African-Americans had to endure to sink in. Wilson successfully intertwines humor, suspense, love, and anger. Production good and Henry Street cast is magnificant--good roles to perform.

R177   Barnes, Clive. "'Seven Guitars' Plucks at those Heartstrings." *New York Post* 29 Mar. 1996: 54.

Wilson is a type of black Chekhov with sadly angry poetry--works of atmosphere, symbols, and characterizations. Play is tighter and cleaner than in Chicago, but needs work. Excellent ensemble performance under Richards, but play wanders and lacks a knockout punch in the last act.

R178   Canby, Vincent. "'Joe Turner' Displays Its Wizardry." *New York Times* 3 Nov. 1996: 5.

Production by New Federal Theater is modest but succeeds in big matters. Like Wilson's other work it is about life, death, and resurrection. Funny, sage, full of love and merciless about "the realities of the human condition." Wilson possesses magic of a wizard and is richest voice in contemporary American theatre. Play is universal, not only speaks for blacks. His works should be done off-Broadway.

R179   Canby, Vincent. "Unrepentant, Defiant Blues for 7 Voices." *New York Times* 29 Mar. 1996: 1C, 32C.

Broadway season only truly begins with *Seven Guitars*, a play of epic proportions and abundant spirit. It is a tightly constructed ensemble piece with conversationsl riffs. Cast superb. Ending muffled, rather than stunning, but Wilson can fix it and the rest of the play is "of such grand design."

R180   Gener, Randy. "Juba to Live." *Village Voice* 26 Nov. 1996: 85.

Says "the joint is jumpin'" with production of *Joe Turner* by a wonderful ensemble company. Comedy present while playwright burrows into tragic material. Jerome Preston Bates attains classical dimensions with an "abysslike sense of loss and barely suppressed rage." Very positive review of play and production.

R181   Jefferson, Margo. "A Song with a Gorgeous First Verse." *New York Times* 21 Apr. 1996: 7H.

An appreciation of Wilson's writing style and the fact that *Seven Guitars* and other works are filled with the spirit of the blues. Writer calls the first act gorgeous and leisurely, with much fine acting. Short second act is hampered by too much of the character Hedley. Feels Richards should have eliminated some problems with the role and the interpretation of it.

R182   Kissel, Howard. "'Guitars' Is Strum-thing to See." *Daily News* 29 Mar. 1996: 1, 49.
            Play is full of quiet truth. First act is pure talk, second with violence which seems artificial. Characters are involving, effect of dialogue is mesmerizing. Play perfectly performed, collaboration of Wilson and Richards unusually powerful in this production.

R183   Lahr, John. "Black and Blues: 'Seven Guitars' a new chapter in August Wilson's ten-play cycle." *New Yorker* 15 Apr. 1996: 99-101.
            Lengthy review of new play plus comments based on interview with Wilson. Importance of the blues in America and in Wilson's plays. Praises the excitement, comedy, and theme of the play. Should win third Pulitzer Prize for Wilson. Acting and directing excellent. Better. than most Broadway shows filled with bogus recipes for happiness.

R184   Lyons, Donald. "Postwar America Today." *Wall Street Journal* 29 Mar. 1996: 7A.
            Seven Guitars is set in the late 1940s. It is a positive joy just to listen to the musicians talking. Wonderful moments throughout and excellent cast. Thinks Wilson has marred play by adding sluggish melodrama, possibly because of previous complaints that his plays are plotless.

R185   Simon, John. "Blue Notes and Blue Ribbons." *New York Magazine* 8 Apr. 1996: 68-69.

First act of *Seven Guitars* beautifully written, poetic, long but never dull. Second act often fails in logic and is frustrating. Thinks Wilson may have tinkered with the play too much. Nevertheless, the play is worth seeing because of strength of much of the writing, the terrific ensemble acting, and the directing by Richards.

R186   "Three Hours in a Pittsburgh Backyard." *Chelsea Clinton News* 11 April 1996: 11.

Feels the play has a lot of "wheel spinning" but is sustained by the fascinating characters and splendid actors performing them. Enjoyable evening for some people, but unreasonable to ask an audience to sit through a play more than three hours. Direction good, acting good, play interesting, but needs cutting.

R187   Van Gelder, Lawrence. "Behind Hardened Hearts, A Fiery Spirit." *New York Times* 23 Oct. 1996: C14.

Play was a highlight of 1988 Broadway season. Many of fine actors in this production veterans of other Wilson plays. The black experience resonates through Wilson's characters. Through the suffering burns a spirit nourished by religion and music and belief in possibilities that may lie down the road. Fine production, excellent actors.

Articles, Chapters, Sections

S188   Barnett, Douglas O. "Up For the Challenge." *American Theatre* Dec. 1996: 60.

A response to August Wilson's comments about casting in the theatre. Says he is a black actor who disagrees with the playwright's viewpoint and who has fought for inclusion in the American theatre. He hopes directors will continue colorblind casting which Wilson criticized in his TCG address. Black actors should not be deprived of the opportunity to act in Shakespeare and Molière and other white playwrights' work because of skin color.

S189   Brantley, Ben. "Women for Whom Speech Is Music." *New York Times* 30 August 1996: C2.

        Urges readers to see *Seven Guitars* because of the three "divas" performing the roles created by Wilson, who "creates the most musical language of any living American playwright." The actresses convey the passion and pain and the sense of the eternal in the everyday in a play which deals with the vital friction of the sexes.

S190   Bellamy, Lou. "Forum." *American Theatre* 9 Nov. 1996: 62, 82.

        Notes his connection with Wilson and their shared views. They both have worked in major regional theatres which he finds it difficult because the assimilation of black art benefits those seeking to admit it more than the black artists. Multicultural efforts of these organizations "often have the effect of destroying black artistic institutions." It is a travesty that no major regional black theatre has been instituted and supported.

S191   "Broadway Tuners Go House-hunting." *Variety* 29 July 1996: n.p.

        Article about profits and losses on recent productions. Gives details about *Seven Guitars*. Says cost $920,000 to produce but must close: it has never found its audience. His plays generate significant income through amateur and regional sales, but commercial tour not likely because already toured.

S192   Brustein, Robert. "Forum." *American Theatre* Nov. 1996: 62, 81.

        Responds to Wilson's letter of Oct. 1996 saying Wilson has stepped back from his extreme separatist position, but is trying to rewrite history. Defends his remarks in the past and continues their debate. He calls Wilson a "race man" and says he is dedicated to "Black Power." Says that Wilson "boasted that he had rejected a well-known and highly respected white director for the film of *Fences*."

S193   Brustein, Robert. "Subsidized Separatism." *American Theatre* October 1996: 26, 27, 100, 101.
                Reprint of the article which first appeared in *New Republic* which is listed below.

S194   Brustein, Robert. "Subsidized Separatism." *New Republic* 19 and 26 Aug. 1996: 39-42.
                A response to August Wilson's keynote address at the TCG Conference published in American Theatre. Says he was misrepresented by Wilson and opposes his views. The speech was a "rambling jeremaid" --the language of self-segregation which he thinks would have surprised Martin Luther King. Asks if a playwright who has had the financial benefits and honors and awards is really in a position "to say blacks are being excluded." His negative criticism of Wilson's plays is aesthetic not racial, sees in them "the monotonous tone of victimization" which is also in his speech.

S195   Evans, Greg. "August a Scorcher at Nonprof Confab." *Variety* 1 July 1996: 45.
                Covers TCG five-day conference, but most of article covers Wilson's speech. He received two standing ovations, but negative reaction to specifics such as no color-blind casting. Criticized "stagnant body of critics" with sharpest criticism for Brustein. Speech eloquent and passionate.

S196   Flatow, Sheryl. "Blues Power." *Playbill* Mar. 1996: 16, 18.
                Article about forthcoming *Seven Guitars* noting the importance of the blues in Wilson's plays and his life. Denies that his plays are formless, says plot points are buried in the language and development of characters. Gives a history of Wilson's career and the enormous success he has had.

S197   Gerstle, Alan. "Not Radical Enough. Forum." *American Theatre* Dec. 1996: 59.

Commentary from a Philadelphia playwright on what he considers "faulty logic and the unfortunate perspective" in Wilson's TCG address. Attacks Wilson for sexist language--always "his" and Wilson's failure to recognize diversity among African-Americans. In a complex and difficult time for theatre, questions of culture and race should be subsumed under broader issues so the struggling theatre community can get a clear vision of its problems.

S198   Grimes, William. "Face to Face on Multiculturalism." *New York Times* 13 Dec. 1996: C2.

Gives a history of the argument between Wilson and Brustein over "black culture, multiculturalism and the theater." Says debate will take place with Anna Deavere Smith as moderator at Town Hall on Jan. 27. Describes Wilson in his TCG address as in a "take no prisoners mood" when atttacking the idea of colorblind casting. Wilson looks forward to the opportunity to broaden the discussion and clarify some things. Brustein and Wilson said they hoped for a reasoned discussion.

S199   Hartigan, Patti. "Forum." *American Theater* Nov. 1996: 63.

A cultural reporter for the *Boston Globe* writes that the argument between Brustein and Wilson is a puerile game between two very big egos. Traces the argument back to 1990 when Brustein "used incendiary language in a negative review of *Fences*." Feels both men are both right and wrong, but the arguments are petty. "If these two men of the *humanities* cannot get beyond their petty differences, what can we hope for as a nation?"

S200   Johann, Susan. "On Listening: An Interview with August Wilson." *American Theatre* April 1996: 22.

Wilson answers questions in a brief interview. Says the Pulitzer Prizes haven't changed him, still considers himself a struggling playwright. Chief influences are Romare Bearden, Amiri Baraka, Jorge Luis

Borges, and the blues. Says writing is both conscious and unconscious.

S201   Krasner, David. "Book Reviews." *Journal of Dramatic Theory and Criticism.* May 1996: 146-50.

A lengthy, close analysis and review of three new books about Wilson. Pereira's 1995 book is described as flawed in failing to consider performances, particularly the work of Richards. It has a high quality of dramaturgical analysis. Shannon's 1995 biocritical study also fails to emphasize performance. She is at her best when "illuminating Wilson's literary skills" and has written a prescient, clear-eyed analysis. Elkins' 1994 collection of ten scholarly essays and interviews is uneven. Krasner discusses each noting the wide range approaches. Says all three books contribute to an understanding of Wilson's work, but there is a need for a performance-oriented study.

S202   Millner, Denene. "One Actor in Tune with 'Seven Guitars.'" *Daily News* 15 April 1996: 34.

Article about Keith David and his successful performance as Floyd Barton in Wilson's play running on Broadway. He plays the role of a guitar player on the verge of success. Preparing for the role in Wilson's musically oriented play required some guitar lessons. Less about the play than his training.

S203   "The Numbers Game." *Variety* 20 May 1966: 43.

Short article about Wilson winning the New York Drama Critics Circle Award for the season's best play. This is the sixth time he has been so honored and has received a check for $1,000. His chief competition was McNally's "Master Class." Critics were divided and three ballots were required before Wilson won.

S204   O'Haire, Patricia. "Tuning Up 'Guitars' for B'way." *Daily News* 27 Mar. 1996: 39.

Wilson is now the only playwright to have all his plays produced on Broadway. Now 50 years old, he is interviewed at favorite coffee shop in New York. Discusses mode of writing plays, need for a woman in *Seven Guitars* initially envisioned as all-male. Wilson now planning his next play set in 1984 about the breakdown in black families.

S205   Purdy, Claude. "Director's Notes." Syracuse *Stage View* Winter/Spring 1996: 2.
          Discusses seeing an exhibit of Romare Bearden's paintings and the impact of "Piano Lesson" on Wilson. The next day Wilson already had characters and was enacting speeches from his future play *The Piano Lesson* which Purdy is directing here as he has previous Wilson plays. Says growing community of people for whom a Wilson play is a "cause for exaltation."

S206   Rosen, Carol. "August Wilson: Bard of the Blues." *Theater Week* 27 May 1996: 18, 20, 22, 24-35.
          Likens him to O'Neill but says Wilson is different in wanting to create a language analogous to the musical language of the blues. Discusses music in each of Wilson's plays. Revealing interview provides material about his work with Richards, future plans, and the history and meaning of *Seven Guitars*. Wilson says his plays are not autobiographical because he is not interested in "small art." New play to be set in 1984 and the joy he finds in writing. Good photos.

S207   Saiz, Laurel. "August Wilson's Journey." Syracuse *Stage View* Winter/Spring 1996: 2.
          Provides a view of Wilson's childhood, his career, and his relationships with various resident theatres in America. Notes that Purdy directed *Fences* for the theatre in 1991. Discusses awards Wilson has won and his role as an African American playwright. Discussion of significance of Wilson's career within American theatre.

S208   Schaefer, Stephen. "Playwright Wilson's Epic Efforts Continue." *New York Post* 27 Mar. 1996: 41.

Brief description of plays from Wilson's cycle for various decades--only three to go [if unpublished *Jitney* one-act is considered] to century's end. Wilson is "amiably modest" for a playwright with titanic ambition. *Seven Guitars* set when Joe Louis retains title and black America was most hopeful. Wilson sticks to theatre despite invitations from Hollywood, although he did write screenplay for *Fences*. Says he hopes it will be filmed.

S209   Schechner, Richard. "Forum." *American Theater* Dec. 1996: 58-59.

Disagrees with only one point in Wilson's TCG speech. He defends color-blind casting and gives positive examples from theatre and opera. Points out that there is no single black culture in America, but a fusion of many. Says casting accorting to racial type is "a stupid, short-sighted and inartistic thing to do." Says in the future white actors without blackface will perform in plays by black playwrights, possibly those by Wilson.

S210   Smith, Dinitia. "A Performance Shaped by Life." *New York Times* 14 May 1996: C13.

Ruben Santiago-Hudson nominated for Canewell in Wilson's "Seven Guitars." Discussion of the play and the character of Canewell. Wilson says the actor "just wears Canewell. He doesn't push him. He just settles in. Canewell is Ruben Santiago-Hudson." Quotes reviews of "Seven Guitars." Says love of language and story telling written by Wilson for Canewell.

S211   Taylor, Regina. "That's Why They Call It the Blues." *American Theatre* April 1996: 18-23.

Analysis of the blues as important in Wilson's life and work, particularly in *Seven Guitars* previewing in New York. The new play is about a blues musician on the verge of success. Calls the play Wilson's most masculine and quotes Wilson saying the play "is about people battling society and themselves for self-worth." Many photos.

S212   Weber, Bruce. "Sculpturing a Play into Existence." New
            York Times 24 Mar. 1996: 7H, 9H.
                    Says critical response to Wilson's plays, more
            than commercial success, has made him attractive to
            producers and investors who want to be associated with
            one of the most important playwrights of our time. Gives
            detailed history of Wilson's cutting and rewriting from
            initial reading at O'Neill Center to final days of rehearsals.
            Excellent plan allows Wilson a sort of "laboratory" for
            theatre art as most playwrights would like to practice it.

S213   Wolf, Matt. "Creating a World: August Wilson's 'Seven
            Guitars.' " *Theatre Today* April 1996: 3-4.
                    Wilson is the only American dramatist whose
            plays are guaranteed a run on Broadway. Notes unusual
            aspect of rich women's roles and how they developed.
            Notes infrequent appearance of whites in Wilson work
            because he does not want to set the plays in a white world.
            His play set in the '80s is about raising children in a world
            with guns and an absence of parental control.

S214   X, Marion. "Forum." *American Theatre* Dec. 1996: 60.
                    Found Wilson's TCG speech puzzling at first, but
            now believes he is stepping out on a limb and asking
            others to follow. Author bemoans the lack of opportunities
            for talented black men and women writers. Asks, "Haven't
            we been around the block enough times to know that no
            one can steal away or deny us our cultural indentity
            without our complicity?" Says expressing one's art in
            culturally specific terms requires courage and conviction.

                                1997

                      Articles, Chapters, Sections

S215   Bruni, Frank. "From the Wings, a Prayer: A Black Troupe
            Improvises." *New York Times* 12 Feb. 1997: C9, 18.

Article about the theatre Wilson singled out in TCG address and debate as a model of what black theatre can and should be. The only black professional resident theatre in the country. Wilson says there should be six or seven like this. Repeats some of Wilson's remarks and responds to them. History of Wilson plays in the theatre. Director Khan does not share Wilson's dislike of black productions of white plays. The company's April 1997 production will be Wilson's early play *Jitney.*

S216   Gates, Jr., Henry Louis, "The Chitlin Circuit." *The New Yorker* 3 Feb. 1997: 44-55.

An important article in reaction to Wilson's TCG speech which the author describes and quotes. Calls Wilson the most celebrated American playwright now writing and says received standing ovation at TCG conference. Notes the speech created immediate controversy. Discusses popular theatre for blacks called "the Chitlin Circuit" in contrast to Wilson's plays which are serious and draw a serious audience--mostly white.

S217   Goldberger, Paul. "From Page to Stage: Race and the Theater." *New York Times* 22 Jan. 1997: C11,14.

A lengthy, close analysis of the forthcoming debate betweeen Brustein and Wilson. Brustein says Wilson's views go against the tradition of integration. Notes that a secondary theme in the debate is the attack on Wilson's plays by Brustein which caused Wilson to lash out at the critic and the fact that Brustein struck back because he had hoped his negative views would have slowed Wilson's "meteoric rise."

S218   Goldstein, Richard. "Culture Shock: The Grudge Match as Kulturkampf." *Village Voice* 28 Jan. 1997: 46-47.

Says 1500 people will gather to see "two eloquent and pompous men duke it out" when Wilson and Brustein debate in Town Hall. Gives a coverage of the causes for the debate and Anna Deavere Smith's interest in arranging it. Notes a production at Yale Rep in 1968 attacked for the representation of blacks which "crystallized Brustein's alienation from radical politics." Discussion of funding for regional theatres and its effect on black artists.

S219   Grimes, William. "Face-to-Face Encounter on Race in the Theater." *New York Times* 29 Jan. 1997: C9-10.
          Coverage of debate sponsored by TCG between Brustein and Wilson. Calls it an evening of passion, principle and drama with paparazzi outside Town Hall, a great crowd, and ticket scalping. Shouted comments at the speakers interrupted them, including "Fascist" shouted at Wilson by a black man. Questions from the audience were answered. No movement together by the two speakers despite efforts by Anna Deavere Smith.

S220   Heilpern, John. "Nobody Wins, Everybody Loses, In Wilson-Brustein Race Debate." *New York Observer* 10 Feb. 1997: 39.
          Coverage of evening saying Wilson impassioned but uncomfortable, Brustein condescending to blacks and whites. Focus on Wilson's views and opposition of many blacks to them. Author agrees with some of playwright's views, but not all. Good overview of whole subject and of the Gates' 1997 article inspired by Wilson's speech. Calls evening a bitter standoff.

S221   Jefferson, Margo. "Oratory vs. Really Talking About Culture." *New York Times* 4 Feb. 1997: C11, 14.
          She found the debate long-winded and disappointing. Brustein cast himself as a lofty ambassador of great Western art. Wilson cast himself as the "warrior king of all people of African descent living in the United States." Neither had the clarity of James Baldwin speaking about culture, nor the interest of a TV program discussing culture. Each man concerned with power to impose his world view on the audience.

S222   Kuhn, Roger S. "Black Theater Debate." *New York Times* 28 Jan. 1997: A20.

Letter to the editor criticizing Brustein for appropriating the memory of Martin Luther King, Jr. in his debate with Wilson. Notes that King argued for black admission into mainstream life, but did not argue for separate cultural institutions as Wilson does today because they had them then--but that was all they had. Nobody can say how King would have viewed the need for black theatre today.

S223   Nesmith, Eugene. "Separate But Equal?" *Village Voice* 11 Feb. 1997: 48.

Analysis of Wilson/Brustein debate which was "sadly lacking in relevant insights." Says American theatre is a history of racism but Brustein refuses to admit it. Argument really boils down to power and values. Writer thinks both men wrong and time for establishment of theatres that are inclusive at every level and reflect the demographics of the world.

S224   Rich, Frank. "Two Mouths Running." *New York Times* 1 Feb. 1997: 19.

Long-time supporter of Wilson describes the debate between him and Brustein as a failure: "two humorless and often petty egomaniacs" repeated their positions. Both ignored larger implications of a crisis in theatre where serious drama "is virtually extinct." Calls the evening tragic because neither man tried to understand the other.

S225   Riedel, Michael. "Guns of August." *Daily News* 26 Jan. 1997: 5.

Wilson's August speech set in motion an argument which will be debated at Town Hall. It promises to be fiery because it seems to be "animated by personal animosity between the playwright and critic. Notes blacks disagree about Wilson's views." Quotes director of Crossroads Theater about casting of blacks and director of Poets Cafe who thinks Wilson is misguided in calling for black theatres because such theatres cannot survive financially.

S226   Serviss, Naomi Freedman. "Wilson Strikes More Than
            Guitar Chords." *Newsday* 10 May 1996: A35.
                 Wilson is giving readings, signing books, and
            relating personal history. Wonderful occasion at the
            Langston Hughes Community Library in one of five
            boroughs he will visit. He spoke about enticing children
            into theatre and teaching them their history. Wilson and
            audience enjoyed presentation which was often humorous.

S227   Silvers, John. "Wilson-Brustein: Whither Multiracial?"
            Back Stage 14 Feb. 1997: 8.
                 A racially mixed actor responds to the debate
            where he asked the first question: where does an actor
            with his mixed heritage fit in? Wilson said he should
            choose a single heritage and express his art through that.
            But Silvers believes in integrating all the aspects of his
            being. Criticism by author of both Brustein and Wilson
            for laying all blame on federal funding policies.

S228   Simon, John. "Black and Blue." *New York Magazine* 17
            Feb. 1997: 57.
                 Short article dismisses event as failing to debate
            important points or maintain interest. Brustein was
            logical, witty and well-informed, Wilson repetitious, self-
            contradictory, and humorless. No examination of black
            theatres and "high" drama Wilson represents. Anna
            Deavere Smith poor moderator: let dialogue wander,
            intruded too much. Whole evening: little wit, less wisdom.

S229   Simonson, Robert. "Wilson v. Brustein: A Drama at Town
            Hall." *Back Stage* 31 Jan. 1997: 3, 41.
                 Long article gives history of the argument
            between Wilson and Brustein and quotes from Wilson's
            TCG speech and Brustein's attack on it. Both men only
            recapitulated this material in the debate. Brustein
            challenged Wilson to premiere one of his plays at an
            African American house or start a black theatre, but
            Wilson answered that he is a playwright and not interested

in starting a theatre. Event was three hours long but only the beginning of a discussion of the points of view.

S230   Solomon, Alisa. "Stock Characters." *Village Voice* 11 Feb. 1997: 46-47.

         "Ballyhooed bout" dull and depressing. Wilson criticizes Brustein, but "his own creaky dramaturgy comes right out of 19th century Europe." Lists playwrights who would have been more meaningful than stock characters: "a onetime Jewish liberal" and "an angry, posturing black man waving the banner of separation as the salvation of the masses, with whom he identifies only romantically."

S231   "Standing Room." *Variety* 2 Feb. 1997: 86.

         Article indicates it is surprising that one of the "hottest tickets in a cold, cold month" would be a showdown between Wilson and Brustein. "Philosophical debate" has been brewing since Wilson "blasted" the nation's theatres for racism at TCG conference. Predicts large audience. Good choice of moderator--Anna Deavere Smith.

S232   Tallmer, Jerry. "A 'Flagship' for Black Theater? Douglas Ward Created It." *The Villager* 5 Feb. 1997: 11.

         Article gives reaction of author and Douglas Ward, co-founder of now defunct Negro Ensemble Company to Wilson's views in debate with Brustein. Author surprised Wilson ignored contributions of Ward. Says Wilson isn't systematic and overlooked history of N.E.C. and is not calling for something new. Wilson is part of the problem--he should write a play for the N.E.C. to produce and bring the company back to life.

S233   "Wilson, Brustein & the Press." *American Theatre* Mar. 1997: 17-19.

         Discussion of debate and reaction to it. Brustein gave appearance of "hip elder intellectual statesman" and maintained real basis of argument goes back to Aristotle and Plato. Wilson in "natty grey suit" like tightly wound spring. He repeated condemnation of current professional theatre scene and much of his TCG speech using impassioned rhetoric to discuss African Americans' needs. Both men were hissed and heckled. Very useful article concludes with excerpts from national press in response to event.

Productions and Credits

The following is a list of major New York productions and key productions at resident theatres throughout the country. The plays have been produced widely throughout the country both in pre-Broadway productions and following the successful New York appearances of the plays. It would be impossible to present information about all the productions. Cast lists are provided, when available, as well as additional information such as production run. In some instances, especially for early productions at resident theatres, it was impossible to get complete information. For each production, a list of reviews cited in the Secondary Bibliography is provided.

P1 *BLACK BART AND THE SACRED HILLS*

P1.1 *Black Bart and the Sacred Hills*. Penumbra Theatre (St. Paul). 10 July-1 Aug. 1982. Directed by Claude Purdy.

P2 *FENCES*

P2.1 *Fences*. Yale Repertory Theatre (New Haven). 30 Apr.-25 May 1985. Directed by Lloyd Richards; setting by James D. Sandefur; costumes by Candice Donnelly; lighting by Danianne Mizzy; music director Dwight Andrews.

      Troy Maxson--James Earl Jones
      Jim Bono--Ray Aranha
      Rose--Mary Alice

        Lyons--Charles Brown
        Gabriel--Russell Costen
        Cory--Cortney B. Vance
        Raynell--Cristal Coleman & LaJara Henderson at alternate
                performances
Reviews: R018, R019, R020.

P2.2 *Fences*. 46th Street Theatre. 26 Mar. 1987. 526 Performances. Directed by Lloyd Richards; setting by James D. Sandefur; costumes by Candice Donnelly; lighting by Danianne Mizzy; music director Dwight Andrews.

        Troy Maxson--James Earl Jones, followed by Billy Dee
                Williams
        Jim Bono--Ray Aranha
        Rose--Mary Alice
        Lyons--Charles Brown
        Gabriel--Frankie R. Faison
        Cory--Courtney B. Vance
        Raynell--Karima Miller
Reviews: R031, R032, R033, R035, R037, R038, R039, R040, R041, R043, R044, R045, R047.

P2.3 *Fences*. 9 May-2 Sept. 1990. Penumbra Theatre Company (St. Paul). Directed by Claude Purdy; setting by W.J.E. Hammer; costumes by Wayne E. Murphey; lighting by Mike Wangen; sound design by Dwight Andrews & Brian J. Peterson.

        Troy Maxson--Lou Bellamy
        Jim Bono--Latifu
        Rose--W. Toni Carter
        Lyons--Terry Bellamy
        Gabriel--Willis Burks
        Cory--Tim Berry
        Raynell--Hanika Alemayehu & Maya J. Beecham at
                alternate performances

P3 *JITNEY*

P3.1 *Jitney*. Penumbra Theatre Company (St. Paul). 13 Dec.-6 Jan. 1984. Directed by Claude Purdy; settings and lights by Scott Peters; costumes by Anna-Marie Mercado; sound design by Lawrence Fried.

> Youngblood--Gregory Williams
> Turnbo--Abdul Razzac
> Fielding--Marion McClinton
> Doub--Latifu
> Shealy--James A. Williams
> Man--Paul Wood
> Becker--Danny Clark
> Rena-- Estelene Bell
> Booster--Terry Bellamy
> Woman--Lisa Carlson

Review: R003.

P4 *JOE TURNER'S COME AND GONE*

P4.1 *Joe Turner's Come and Gone*. Yale Repertory Theatre (New Haven). 29 Apr.-24 May 1986. Directed by Lloyd Richards; setting by Scott Bradley; costumes by Pamela Peterson; lighting by Michael Gianitti; musical direction by Dwight Andrews; sound design by Matthew Wiener.

> Seth Holly--Mel Winkler
> Bertha Holly--L. Scott Caldwell
> Bynum Walker--Ed Hall
> Rutherford Selig--Raynor Scheine
> Jeremy Furlow--Bo Rucker
> Herald Loomis--Charles S. Dutton
> Zonia Loomis--Cristal Coleman and LaJara Henderson at
> alternate performances
> Mattie Campbell--Kimberly Burroughs
> Rueben Mercer--Casey Lydell Badger and LaMar James
> Fedrick at alternate performances
> Molly Cunningham--Kimberly Scott
> Martha Pentecost--Angela Bassett

Reviews: R024, R025, R026.

P4.2 *Joe Turner's Come and Gone*. Arena Stage (Washington). 2 Oct. 1987. Yale Repertory Theatre Production; directed by Lloyd Richards; setting by Scott Bradley; costumes by Pamela Peterson; lighting by Michael Gianitti; musical direction--Dwight Andrews.

> Seth Holly--Mel Winkler
> Bertha Holly--L. Scott Caldwell
> Bynum Walker--Ed Hall
> Rutherford Selig--Raynor Scheine
> Jeremy Furlow--Bo Rucker
> Herald Loomis--Delroy Lindo
> Zonia Loomis--Kippen Hay and Kellie S. Williams at alternate performances
> Mattie Campbell--Kimberleigh Aarn
> Reuben Mercer--LaFontaine Oliver and Vincent Prevost at alternate performances
> Molly Cunningham--Kimberly Scott
> Martha Pentecost--Angela Bassett

P4.3 *Joe Turner's Come and Gone*. Ethel Barrymore Theatre. 26 Mar. 1988. 105 Performances. Directed by Lloyd Richards; setting by Scott Bradley; costumes by Pamela Peterson; lighting by Michael Gianitti; musical direction by Dwight Andrews.

> Seth Holly--Mel Winkler
> Bertha Holly--L. Scott Caldwell
> Bynum Walker--Ed Hall
> Rutherford Selig--Raynor Scheine
> Jeremy Furlow--Bo Rucker
> Herald Loomis--Delry Lindo
> Zonia Loomis--Jamila Perry
> Mattie Campbell--Kimberly Aarn
> Reuben Mercer--Richard Parnell Habersham
> Molly Cunningham--Kimberly Scott
> Martha Pentecost--Angela Bassett

Reviews: R063, R064, R065, R066, R067, R068, R069, R070, R071, R072.

P4.4 *Joe Turner's Come and Gone*. 8 May-21 July 1991. Penumbra Theatre Company (St. Paul). Directed by Claude Purdy; setting by W.J.E. Hammer; costumes by Ainsley Bruneau; lighting by Mike Wangen; sound design by Dwight D. Andrews; with Adbul Salaam El Razzac, Lou Bellamy, and Sandi Ross.

P4.5 *Joe Turner's Come and Gone*. 16 Oct.- 1 Dec. 1996. New Federal Theatre (New York). Directed by Clinton Turner Davis. Setting by Felix E. Cochren; costumes by Vassie Welbeck-Browne; lighting by Shirley Prendergast; music by Todd Borton.

> Seth Holly--Mike Hodge
> Bertha Holly--Peggy Alston
> Bynum Walker--Arthur French
> Rutherford Selig--Ron Riley
> Jeremy Furlow--Chad L. Coleman
> Harold Loomis--Jerome Preston Bates
> Zonia Loomis--Sharia Rashed
> Mattie Campbell--Joyce Lee
> Reuben Mercer--Aaron Deener
> Molly Cunningham--Caroline Stefanie Clay
> Martha Pentecost--Kim Yanzey Moore

Reviews: R176, R178, R180, R187.

P5 *MA RAINEY'S BLACK BOTTOM*

P5.1 *Ma Rainey's Black Bottom*. Yale Repertory Theatre (New Haven). 6-21 Apr. 1984. Directed by Lloyd Richards; settings by Charles Henry McClennahan; costumes by Daphne Pascucci; lighting by Peter Maradudin; musical direction by Dwight Andrews.

> Sturdyvant--Richard M. Davidson
> Irvin--Lou Criscuolo
> Cutler--Joe Seneca
> Toledo--Robert Judd
> Slow Drag--Leonard Jackson
> Levee--Charles S. Dutton
> Ma Rainey--Theresa Merritt
> Policeman--David Wayne Nelson
> Dussie Mae--Sharon Mitchell
> Sylvester--Steven R. Blye

Reviews: R007, R011.

P5.2 *Ma Rainey's Black Bottom.* Cort Theatre. 11 Oct. 1984. 275 Performances. Directed by Lloyd Richards; settings by Charles Henry McClennahan; costumes by Daphne Pascucci; lighting by Peter Maradudin; musical direction by Dwight Andrews.

> Sturdyvant--John Carpenter
> Irvin--Lou Criscuolo
> Cutler--Joe Seneca
> Toledo--Robert Judd
> Slow Drag--Leonard Jackson
> Levee--Charles S. Dutton
> Ma Rainey--Theresa Merritt
> Policeman--Christopher Loomis
> Dussie Mae--Aleta Mitchell
> Sylvester--Scott Davenport-Richards

Reviews: R001, R002, R004, R005, R006, R008, R009, R010, R012, R013.

P5.3 *Ma Rainey's Black Bottom.* Penumbra Theatre Company (St. Paul). 7-31 May 1987. Directed by Claude Purdy; setting by W.J.E. Hammer; costumes by Deidrea Whitlock; lighting by Scott Peters; sound design by Dwight Andrews.

> Sturdyvant--Jack Walsh
> Irvin--Peter Maronge
> Cutler--Danny Clark
> Toledo--Marion McClinton
> Slow Drag--Otis Montgomery
> Levee--Terry Bellamy
> Ma Rainey--Edna Duncan
> Dussie Mae--Estelene Bell
> Sylvester--David Earl Williams
> Policeman--Joseph Melich

Reviews: R034, R036.

P6 *MALCOLM X*

P6.1 *Malcolm X.* Penumbra Theatre Company (St. Paul). Directed by Claude Purdy. Written by Wilson for touring company, performs occasionally in different locations with different actors. Was performed at first National Black Theatre Festival in 1991.

P7 *THE PIANO LESSON*

P7.1 *The Piano Lesson*. Yale Repertory Theatre (New Haven). 26 Nov.-19 Dec. 1987. Directed by Lloyd Richards; setting by E. David Cosier, Jr.; costumes by Constanza Romero; lighting design by Christopher Akerlind; musical direction by Dwight Andrews; sound design by J. Scott Servheen.

> Doaker--Carl Gordon
> Boy Willie--Samuel L. Jackson
> Lymon--Rocky Carroll
> Berniece--Starletta DuPois
> Maretha--Chenee Johnson and Ylonda Powell at alternate
>   performances
> Avery--Tommy Hollis
> Wining Boy--Lou Myers
> Grace--Sharon Washington

Reviews: R042, R046.

P7.2 *The Piano Lesson*. Huntington Theatre (Boston). 9 Jan. 1988. Yale Repertory Theatre Production. Directed by Lloyd Richards; setting by E. David Cozier, Jr.; costumes by Constanza Romero; lighting by Christopher Akerlind; musical direction by Dwight Andrews; sound design by J. Scott Servheen.

> Doaker--Carl Gordon
> Boy Willie--Carles S. Dutton
> Lymon--Rocky Carroll
> Berniece--Starletta DuPois
> Maretha--Jaye Skinner
> Avery--Tommy Hollis
> Wining Boy--Lou Myers
> Grace--Sharon Washington

P7.3 *The Piano Lesson*. Walter Kerr Theatre. 16 Apr. 1990.   329 Performances. Directed by Lloyd Richards; settings by E. David Cosier, Jr.; costumes by Constanza Romero; lighting design; Christopher Akerlind;

musical direction by Dwight D. Andrews; sound design by G. Thomas Clark.

> Doaker--Carl Gordon
> Boy Willie--Charles S. Dutton
> Lymon--Rocky Carroll
> Berniece--S. Epatha Merkerson
> Maretha--Apryl R. Foster
> Avery--Tommy Hollis
> Wining Boy--Lou Myers
> Grace--Lisa Gay Hamilton

Reviews: R090, R091, R092, R094, R095, R096, R097, R098, R100, R102, R103, R104.

P7.4 *The Piano Lesson*. Grandel Square Theatre (St. Louis). Produced by the St. Louis Black Repertory Theatre. 12 Sept.-11 Oct. 1992. Lighting by Kathy A. Perkins; costumes by Antonitta Barnes.

> Doaker--Ron Himes
> Boy Willie--Cedric Turner
> Lymon--Darrell Rutlin
> Berniece--Linda Kennedy
> Maretha--Danielle Pryor
> Wining Boy--Bus Howard

P7.5 *The Piano Lesson*. Theatre Three (Dallas). 20 Oct.-15 Nov. 1992. Directed by Laurence O'Dwyer.

> Doaker--Willie Minor
> Boy Willie--Richard Ridley
> Avery--Lloyd Barnes

P7.6 *The Piano Lesson*. Penumbra Theatre Company (St. Paul). 5 May -18 July 1993. Directed by Marion McClinton; setting by W.J.E. Hammer; costumes by Anne Ruben; lighting by Mike Wangen; music direction by Kevin Jackson; sound design by Terry Tilley.

> Doaker--Lou Bellamy
> Boy Willie--William Wilkins
> Lymon--Lester Purry
> Berniece--Rebecca Rice
> Maretha--Livia Hoskins & Shali Williams at alternate
>   performances

Avery--Terry Bellamy
Wining Boy--Willis Burks
Grace--Tonia Jackson

Reviews: R144, R151.

P7.7 *The Piano Lesson*. Syracuse Stage. 27 Feb. 1996. Directed by Claude Purdy; setting by Donald Eastman; costumes by Maria Marrero; lighting design by Phil Monat; sound design by James Wildman.

Doaker--Robert Colston
Boy Willie--Alex Allen Morris
Lymon--Terence Rosemore
Berniece--Ami Brabson
Maretha--Shekinah "Glory" Marie Brown and Maleah Seals
at alternate performances
Avery--Allie Woods, Jr.
Wining Boy--Jim Ponds
Grace--Natasha Welch

P8 *SEVEN GUITARS*

P8.1 *Seven Guitars*. Goodman Theatre (Chicago). 1 Feb.-25 Feb. 1995. Directed by Walter Dallas; setting by Scott Bradley; costumes by Constanza Romero; lighting by Christopher Akerlind; with Jerome Preston Bates, Viola Davis, Rosalyn Coleman, Tommy Hollis, Ruben Santiago-Hudson, and Michele Shay.
Reviews: R167, R169, R170, R172.

P8.2 *Seven Guitars*. Walter Kerr Theatre. Mar. 28 1996. Directed by Lloyd Richards; setting by Scott Bradley; costumes by Constanza Romero; lighting by Christopher Akerlind, sound by Tom Clark.

Floyd--Keith David
Vera--Viola Davis
Ruby--Rosalyn Coleman
Red Carter--Tommy Hollis
Canewell--Ruben Santiago-Hudson
Louise--Michele Shay
Hedley--Roger Robinson

Reviews: R177, R179, R181, R182, R183, R184, R185, R186.

P9 *TWO TRAINS RUNNING*

P9.1 *Two Trains Running.* Yale Repertory Theatre (New Haven). 27 Mar.-21 Apr. 1990. Directed by Lloyd Richards; setting by Tony Fanning; costumes by Chrisi Karvonides; lighting by Geoff Korf; sound design by Ann Johnson.

> Memphis--Al White
> Wolf--Samuel L. Jackson
> Risa--Ella Joyce
> Holloway--Samuel E. Wright
> Sterling--Larry Fishburne
> Hambone--Sullivan Walker
> West--Leonard Parker

Reviews: R097, R099, R101.

P9.2 *Two Trains Running.* Walter Kerr Theatre. 13 Apr. 1992. Directed by Lloyd Richards; setting by Tony Fanning; costumes by Chrisi Karvonides; lighting by Geoff Korf.

> Memphis--Al White
> Wolf--Anthony Chisholm
> Risa--Cynthia Martells
> Holloway--Roscoe Lee Browne
> Sterling--Larry Fishburne
> Hambone--Sullivan Walker
> West--Chuck Patterson

Reviews: R123, R124, R125, R126, R127, R128, R129, R130, R131, R132, R133, R134.

P9.3 *Two Trains Running.* Goodman Theatre (Chicago). 25 Jan.-28 Feb. 1993. Moved to New Regal Theatre (Chicago) 4-14 Mar. 1993. Directed by Lloyd Richards; setting by Tony Fanning; costumes by Chrisi Karvonides; lighting by Geoff Korf.

> Memphis--Paul Butler
> Wolf--Anthony Chisholm
> Risa--Bellary Darden
> Holloway--Roscoe Lee Browne
> Sterling--Eriq La Salle
> Hambone--Lou Ferguson
> West--John Beasley

Reviews: R146, R147, R152.

P9.4 *Two Trains Running.* Penumbra Theatre Company. 4 May-12 June 1994. Directed by Marion McClinton; setting by W.J.E. Hammer; costumes by Robin Murray; lighting by Mike Wangen; sound design by John Simms; with David Alan Anderson, Terry Bellamy, James Craven, Marvette Knight, Lester Purry, Omari Shakir, and Adolphus Ward.
Reviews: R157, R158.

Author Index

The following index lists all critics and scholars included in the secondary bibliographies. The references are keyed to the numbers ("R"= reviews; "S" = books, articles, sections) assigned to the entries.

General Index

The following index records page references as well as references keyed to the primary ("A"= non-dramatic references) and secondary ("P" = productions and credits; "R"= reviews; "S" = books, articles and sections) bibliographies.

About the Author

YVONNE SHAFER is Professor in the Humanities Division of St. John's University, Staten Island. She has taught at numerous universities in the United States, Europe, and China and was a Fulbright Professor in Brussels. She has published several books and her articles have appeared in numerous journals.

ISBN 0-313-29270-1